HOUSECAT CONFIDENTIAL

By

Fin & Meg S. Hart

Copyright © 2010 by Fin & Meg S. Hart

All rights reserved. Except as permitted under the U.S. Copyright Act of 1976, no part of this publication may be reproduced, distributed, or transmitted in any form or by any means, or stored in a database or retrieval system, without the prior written permission of the author.

Authors: Fin & Meg S. Hart

Visit us online at www.housecatconfidential.com

Cover Design by Debbie Glovatsky
Interior Photography by Meg S Hart

ISBN: 1452802254
EAN-13: 9781452802251

THE SECRET OF LIFE

Hello, dear readers. My name is Fin, although I'm known by many names – Finny, Finny de Floof, and Speed Bump, to name a few.

I'm a grannycat, a senior kitizen, but I don't mind getting older. I can't jump like a kitten anymore, but I haven't just grown older, I've also grown wiser. I have so much wisdom I want to share with humans and kitties alike. I've discovered the secret of life and I want to share it with all of you. Why don't we curl up on the couch together and I'll tell you everything I've learned.

Wait; is that someone in the kitchen, by the can opener? Oh, it is, I gotta go!

Sorry about that. What a disappointment, it was only a can of corn. Oh nibblets, how you mock me.

Now where was I? Oh no, now I've lost my train of thought. I guess I'll just start at the beginning and I'm sure it'll come back to me.

Fin & Hart

Housecat Confidential

May I speak frankly?

Fin & Hart

BEGININGS

"Hey, big floofy girl!" My brother Archie taunted, as our other siblings all turned to see the fight brewing between us. Our arguments had become the daily floor show in the small room we lived in at the animal shelter. "You gave *our* Mom another hairball!"

"What? No I didn't!" I yelled back, my tail puffing in defense.

It wasn't uncommon for Archie the Horrible to be cruel to one of us, but I was the only one who dared to fight back. I was busy thinking of an insult to put him back in his place, when I replayed his comment in my head.

"What do you mean by *our* Mom? She's my Mom too."

"Are you sure about that, Big Floofy Girl?" He said with a sneer. "I mean, it's not like you look like the rest of us. Mom's a short-haired grey tabby cat like us, and you're, well, you…"

I could hear the other kittens gasp at his forwardness. It was as if he had finally acknowledged the elephant in the middle of the room. I could tell by the uncomfortable silence, and the fact that none of them would return my gaze, that they'd all be thinking it, even if they'd had the good sense to not bring it up.

It had always been obvious to me that I was different from my brothers and sisters, but until that moment, I'd loved all the things that made me stand out. I was a bit larger than the others, I have the white blaze on my nose that runs all the way down my tummy, and my white boots – but it was my long floofy fur that had made me a regular target of Archie's attacks.

"I'm a tabby too. See the tabby mask around my eyes, and my tabby cuffs!" I said, stretching out my front paws to display my tabby stripes with pride. I was certain this would shut him up. He was usually all meow and no bite.

"Yeah, but what about your little white boots?" He said with a cruel snicker. At that moment, I wanted to use one of my white boots to whap him right in the chops.

"Well, maybe Dad was a white boy," I said defending my honor. "Look at Snow, she's all white – no tabby markings at all!" I pointed to the other black sheep in our little family, my all white sister. I did feel a little bit bad for calling her out, but everyone loved Snow. I knew they'd never turn on her.

"What about the solid black patches on the back of your legs?" Snow said, defending her place in the family.

I'm not sure what was more shocking at that moment – Snow seemingly taking Archie's side or the fact that I had black patches on the backs of my legs. It took all I had not to flop on the floor and have a look, but even as a kitten I knew this was no time for distraction.

"Plus I have short fur like Mom," Snow said, her face clearly indicating she had taken up a side that wasn't mine in this battle. She was on my list now too.

"And look at those giant paws! They're like snow shoes with all that floofy fur!" Archie said.

"Shut up Archibaldy!" I yelled, calling attention to the small bald spot above his ears. Sure it was mean, but not undeserved.

At this moment Mother Tabby was brought back into our room. She had been taken away briefly to be checked out after the hairball incident. To avoid scolding, we all dispersed to neutral corners. No one came to be in mine. I never felt so alone. Maybe I really wasn't a part of this family.

It wasn't long before we all settled in for lunch at Mom's belly buffet. I'll admit to taking my "large" back paw and shoving Archie out of the way with it. I drank a good portion of his share of milk too – big floofy girls need to keep up their strength after all.

Mom must have heard what happened from one of the other kittens. Maybe she just noticed I was a bit sad that afternoon and was staying to myself, because she made a special effort to come over and snuggle with me.

"Are you okay, Sweetie?" She asked, as she rubbed her head against mine.

"Mom, am I really your kitten?" I asked, barely able to keep my voice steady. I held my breath as I waited. Her face said it all.

"I love you with all my heart," she said, her eyes glistening with emotion, but we both noticed she failed to answer the question. "Come here Sweetie, and let me clean your ears." I settled down on her front paws for a bath.

As she cleaned my ears and licked my head she whispered to me about her addiction to catnip and stories of wild nights on the streets of Sin City that she could barely recall.

Mother Tabby had been a housecat at one time, but through circumstances she didn't understand she had become homeless. She was living on the streets when she was knocked up with kitten. She was rescued and brought to a shelter, right before she gave birth. She explained that it was a confusing time for her. She was disoriented with the new surroundings and all the people. Living as a stray for such a long time she'd become more wary of humans.

"Next thing I knew I was giving you all a lick bath," she said. "I have to admit it's possible that you were brought in from another litter, but I loved you the minute I saw you. I've always thought of you as one of my own, even if you aren't." Her beautiful green eyes filled with tears and she purred from deep down. "I've never noticed the length of your fur – I just feel the love in my heart. It's love that makes you one of my babies."

I still love her for that.

It made me realize that family is about a lot more than blood.

Once the shock wore off, I began to construct a history for myself that might include being the offspring of feline royalty. I know what you're thinking, but a whole land is named after me (you know Fin-Land). I embraced my uniqueness and knew it would help get me a wonderful family when the time came.

I never doubted I would find a home with a human family.

As the time for our adoption grew closer I became nervous and excited. I wondered how it would happen. Would I know the minute I saw them? Would I be a second cat or an only cat?

Mother Tabby had explained to us how great a human home could be for a cat. "It's the best possible gig." She'd say. "Some housecats are treated like royalty by their humans and are given treats on command!" It sounded like heaven to me.

While some of my siblings looked out the windows with longing, dreaming of a life on the outside, I knew Mother Tabby was right – housecat was the best possible outcome.

As it turns out, not everyone wants a floofy cat, a fact I learned when the first families came in to adopt us.

"Not that one, it'll shed!" I overheard one of the potential family members say when they visited the shelter.

"Its hairs are like a raccoon, they'll show on everything!" Another exclaimed.

It was a hard lesson, but I always kept my faith. At some level I must have known my human parents were pining away for me, long before they even met me.

Housecat Confidential

Go ahead, smooch the page if you need too.

Fin & Hart

THE KITTEN HUNT

As I was waiting to meet my future human family, it turns out they were just as anxious to meet me. Mom was finally past the grief of losing her precious cat Kirin, and she desperately wanted a new kitten. She had convinced my future Dad that a new kitten was just what they needed. He knew it was a battle he was not going to win.

They quickly discovered that (at least here in the desert) there are seasons when kittens are readily available and seasons when kittens are actually quite scarce. Unfortunately they'd chosen a time to be ready when kittens were very hard to find.

Mom told me about all the crazy things she did to find me. She said she called the local pet stores and shelters so often they knew her by voice alone. She admitted to doing what any kitten-hungry woman would do; disguising her voice with fake accents, English one week or Southern the next.

Mom had a kitten calendar she would fawn over while searching for me. It was filled with pictures of furry cuties. She loved the photos of the Norwegian Forest Cats and Maine Coons but Dad had insisted he didn't want a long-haired cat (too much shedding, he said). She'd move on to the photos of the sweet white and grey tabby kittens which she also loved. One of those would be perfect too, she'd think.

One Saturday in February, after she'd tried all her regular kitten haunts, and was ready to call it quits, she picked up the classifieds from the local paper, and spotted this:

"Grey tabby kittens, $50 each. Call 555-****."

She couldn't believe her luck, kittens at last, and grey tabbies even. It was a small shelter way across town, and one she'd never heard of. She told me she tried to remain calm as she dialed, maybe we'd be gone already.

"Do you still have the kittens!?" She'd practically shouted when the shelter owner finally answered the phone.

"Yeah, there are about five of them. Grey tabby cats and one little white one."

"Do you have any females?"

"I think so – the white one's a girl for sure."

"I'm on my way! Can you hold a girl tabby for me?"

"Uh, sure lady…"

She didn't wait for Dad to come home from work. She didn't even wait to get him on the phone to say she was going to look. She was too afraid someone would come and scoop us all up and her kitten search would have to continue.

She tells me her heart was racing in her chest as she walked into the small room where we were all being kept. Would she know her future cat as soon as she saw her? She always knew before, within a few minutes.

Her eyes settled on me immediately; she always tells me it was love at first sight. It was love at first sight for me too. She had kind eyes, an ample lap for napping, and she smelled like what I thought Home should smell like.

She was also a long hair, and I just knew she wouldn't judge me. I rightly sensed she was a shedder too.

"Dibs!" I called out, so no one else would try to claim her for themselves; competition for a great home was fierce among us kittens.

"Aren't you the cutest kitten in the world?" she asked in a high-pitched squeal as she clapped her hands over her mouth. "Oh, but your Dad said no long hairs!"

It was clear she wanted to betray that request. She just needed some help.

I was so nervous when she started to play it cool with me, especially after that first squeal of delight. To my horror, she picked up Archibaldy and gave him a look over. She quickly discarded him when she determined he was a boy (they'd agreed a girl was the only way to go).

Even Snow tried her best efforts to get in my future mother's lap and win her over. I had to clock Snow with my front paw to stop her (I know what you're thinking, but honestly, she deserved it; I'd called dibs after all – this human was mine). It made Mom laugh, and knew I was winning her over.

Mom picked up a string toy and began swinging it around to play with us. I loved the way she moved it (first on the floor and then over the sparse furniture in our room, making for a fine chase). I liked how she tried to make it challenging, but not too challenging, like she wanted me to catch it.

I leaped the highest and chased the hardest in order to impress her. She would clap with delight at each acrobatic feat. Finally she couldn't resist me any longer and scooped me up.

"Okay little one, if you're a girl – you're mine!" She called the owner of the shelter over to verify my sex, and then the real snuggling commenced.

She cooed and I purred. It was real love all right.

She was still a bit worried Dad might be unhappy about the long-hair situation because she actually asked if I could be exchanged if he was displeased. Hmm, guess she didn't realize this inquiry would be displeasing to me. I forgave her though, since we were in love.

Housecat Confidential

Mom got busy paying the check to spring me from the shelter. While she was filling out the paperwork, I focused all my attention on trying to eat the floral arrangement on the desk, and then batting the pen Mom used as she wrote the check. I was easily distracted as a kitten – I was all play back then.

Once the paperwork was completed, and Mom had me in her arms, I suddenly realized I'd be leaving my feline family forever. My time with Mother Tabby was ending, and she had been the best mom a kitten could ask for. As for my siblings, regardless of the harsh words between us, I loved all of my family (even Archie and Snow) and knew I'd miss them.

I flailed free of Mom's grasp and clawed my way up to her shoulder for one last look. Mother Tabby's eyes were filled with pride and a touch of sadness.

I called out to them, sending them all my best wishes for a long and happy life. I hope with all my heart it happened for each one of them, but especially for Mother Tabby. I hope she is a fat and sassy housecat living the life she had dreamed of for each of us.

"Okay sweetie, let's get you home," Mom said as she plucked me from her shoulder and held me close to her chest as we headed out to the car.

"Hey, wanna go meet your new Dad first?" She said as she stopped and held me up to her face.

Maybe she saw my look of trepidation because she showered me with chin scritches. "Don't worry. I think he'll fall in love with you as soon as he sees you."

She got into the car and plunked me down in her lap, but that was clearly not going to work. I was too excited and too curious. I scaled the seat and leaped onto the head rest to taste her hair. It was, and still is, yummy.

"Oh my! You're not going to sit still are you?"

"Mew!" I confirmed and made a break for the wide open of the backseat. She caught me mid-leap with one hand and pulled me back to her chest.

Seemed that in her rush to leave the house, she hadn't really planned on how she was going to safely transport me.

She held me close to her chest as she dug through the trunk of her car, while I batted her hair. She finally discovered a lidless cardboard box. She tried just putting me in it on the front seat, but of course that was no good either. I wanted to be everywhere, including under her feet as she tried to drive.

She finally got the idea of turning the box over on top of me as I sat on the front seat, trapping me inside like a prisoner. Where was the dignity? I had my complaints which I was only too happy to voice.

"I'm sorry but we have to be safe," she explained.

I appreciated her concern and quieted down for the trip. She tried to make me feel safe and loved, right from the start. She told me how much they wanted me in their family and how long and hard they'd searched.

I was still nervous about meeting Dad, worried he might reject me. I couldn't imagine having to go back to the shelter now. I hadn't even seen my house yet but I knew I was where I belonged. I didn't know it at the time, but Mom would have fought with all she had to keep me. It was like that with us from the start.

What felt like days later (Mom drives like a little old lady), she finally arrived at Dad's work. She pulled into the parking lot and tooted the horn to catch his attention. He came out to the car to see why she was visiting.

"What are you doing here?" He asked as he opened the passenger's door.

"I found our cat," she said proudly as she uncovered the box to reveal me beneath it. We both held our breath as Dad took me in with his eyes, and then his heart.

"Oh my goodness!" he said, as he clapped his hands over his mouth to cover a little delighted squeal.

Dad had never really been a "cat person" until he saw me beneath that box, and then he was a total convert. He says I looked like an adorable, powder puff with huge eyes. I loved him immediately. He's so funny and he has happy eyes. I could tell he would play with me and be a great petter.

He took me into his office without even waiting for Mom to get out of the car. He let me explore the office as he looked on, beaming – seemed the long-hair wasn't going to be a problem after all; no exchange was going to be required. I think that's when I officially became a "Daddy's Girl."

I explored the whole place, thinking it might be my new home. It seemed a bit sterile but as long as they were there it would be the best home ever. He put me up on his desk and I sat down next to his can of cola.

"She's barely taller than the can!" he said looking for his Polaroid camera to take my first family photo. The picture came out awful (the first of many bad photos taken by my parents). It's too blurry to tell but I was beaming.

Dad secured a better transport box (one with a lid) and finally allowed Mom to take me to our home, My New Home.

"It's kinda small but I really hope you like it," Mom said as she took me from my transport box and carefully placed me on the floor of the laundry room. I could tell she wanted to hold me forever, but that wasn't going to be possible (I like to flail when held).

"This is gonna be where your litter box will go," she said pointing to the little doorway that was cut into the lower cabinet door. "Gosh, I hope your Dad remembers to pick up a litter box at the pet store."

We exchanged a short look of concern, both hoping she was right about Dad remembering this critical purchase. She also worried for a moment that I might not be able to get in and out. She opened the door and plopped me down and shut the door behind me. I was quick to leap out of the door. Getting into the cabinet was a bit trickier, but with a few scrambles with my back paws I was in and out without any trouble.

Hey, what's this thing with an open door? I wondered as I tried to climb up its smooth metal surface, to the mysterious hole in the middle.

"No, don't get in the dryer – that's a NO-NO!"

And so began my parents' love affair with the word "No" used in conversations directed at me – for awhile I thought it might become my name. Of course I understood what the word meant. I didn't understand all human speech back then, but I knew that one – just chose to ignore it – and still do.

Next on the tour was the hallway – ah the hallway. I didn't yet see the strategic advantage of the hallway. Later I'd learn it's a great place to keep my eyes on the comings and goings of my parents. Sure they complain about my being in their way, but it's my house too.

"Meow?" I inquired about the room to the left.

"That's your Dad's office, and through the far door is the living room."

I was going to head into the office, until I saw the room to the right. It stopped me dead in my tracks. Are those ribbons and feathers?

"Oh that's my art studio," Mom said with obvious pride. "Your Dad calls it my crap, er craft room. I'm not sure you should go in there though."

Naturally I ignored her and headed right in. The long ribbons hanging off the edge of the desk were the first things that drew me, and Mom frantically trying to roll them up only made it that much more fun.

The art paper was next. Ah, so satisfying to claw and nibble on.

"No, no. Don't claw those!" Mom said as she scooped me up with one hand and shoved the papers in a drawer with the other.

At this point I was escorted from the room and she shut the door behind us. I began marking the hours until I would return unsupervised. I love that room – all those things to play with and it has a perfect mid-morning patch of sun.

"You wanna get down now?" Mom asked as I flailed about in her arms. "Okay, okay. Watch the claws."

I stopped to paw at the door which I was told was the hall closet. I didn't know it then, but it's the lair of the Evil Dyson. I'm sure she didn't want to scare me.

The hall bath wasn't too exciting – yet. I was too small to leap onto the things I'd later come to love. It's also home to the tall water bowl my parents sit on. I don't use this water bowl to much anymore because it's become more difficult to perch. I like to sit on the counter too. It's great to have a face to face chat with Mom while she sits in there. I like it when we can be at eye level.

"That's our bedroom, Boots." We exchanged a glance and decided immediately that would not be my name – bad Archie memories. "Oh NO, don't go under there!"

I barely heard her as I raced under the bed. It's quite tall which I love. I realized I could hang out under there, while Mom was unable to get under it at all. In fact, even today, I can sit under the bed, square in the middle, and not be easily reached from any side (perfect for when I've been naughty).

The walk-in closet is also delightful. It's filled with secret places where even my parents can't find me (like behind the laundry basket – hmm, guess that one isn't a secret anymore; think I'll keep the others to myself).

The living/dining room combination turned out to be a real misnomer because oddly enough, no one lives in or dines there. It's an activity wasteland. Even now I rarely play there, oh except on the dining table when no one is looking.

Finally there was the den/kitchen combination called the "Great Room" and it is great. Great because it's where my parents like to hang out the most – and because it's where my food and water dishes are kept.

I was very pleased with the place. It was just what Mother Tabby had dreamed of for us. There was a yard to explore too, but I was pretty tired by then, so I just took a peak through the window on the back door. We settled down for a good snuggle while we waited for Dad's arrival.

"You feel like mink," Mom said as she petted me. I still don't know what mink feels like, but my fur is silky soft and luxurious.

"And these paws! You even have long-hair between your toes!" She said as her voice rose into a squeal. I made it clear the rear paws were off limits, but I allow front paw holding.

Meanwhile Dad stopped at Petsmart on the way home and went all out to spoil me with lots of toys and goodies. When our little family was all together again I was drunk with happiness (and a touch of the catnip from the new toys, if truth be told).

"What should we do with her?" Dad asked and it stopped my heart for just a moment until he finished with "You know, while we're sleeping."

"She'll sleep with us."

"She's so tiny. What if we roll over on her in our sleep?" I don't think he'd ever been around such a small animal. "What about setting up a little bed on the floor?"

"I guess – but I don't think she's gonna go for that."

They set up a special box, with a pillow in it on the bedroom floor, and we all settled in for the night. I was very small and our bed is very tall, but Mom was right, I didn't want to be away from them on my first night (or any night after).

I climbed up the steep, sheer cliff to get to them, my claws digging into the comforter like a mountain climber. Once I reached the top I marched right down the center of the bed until I reached their sleeping heads.

"Meow!" I said to let them know, right up front, that access wouldn't be denied.

"She's like a tiger with that big set of lungs! Maybe we should call her Tiger?" Dad said as he laughed and smothered me with pets.

"No. She's not a Tiger," Mom said as I took the place of honor between their pillows.

"Me-ah-ma" I said, settling on my name for my lady parent. This is loosely translated into "enjoyable lap and generous treater" or "Lapper" for short.

"Did you hear that? I think she called me Mom!"

"Me-ah-ma" I repeated, correcting her, but gave in eventually and let her go with the more human sounding "Mom."

"So it's over – The Kitten Hunt?" Aow said, although he knew the answer already. Oh that's Dad's name in cat. It's loosely translated into "firm petter, provides table scraps" or "Scrapper" for short.

"C'est Fini," Mom said as she looked at me with adoration. It made both Dad and me perk up at the words.

"What's that mean?"

Fin & Hart

"It means "It's Finished" in French… at least I think so." Yeah don't be too impressed with the French thing, turns out she only remembers about ten words, twenty if you count food, and back to seven if spelling counts. "Hey, Fini would be a cute name for her!"

"How about just – Fin?"

"I love that. I think it means "The End" in French, like they roll at the end of a French movie"

Really it was just the beginning.

Housecat Confidential

Fin & Hart

DADDY'S GIRL

Let me start by saying unequivocally that I love Mom. I know she loves me no matter what, when I'm naughty or cross, and even when I nibble on her (okay, technically it's biting – I know I shouldn't, but she just tastes so yummy). Whatever I do, I know she loves me.

I also have to admit that from the start I've had a special bond with Dad. I feel like I've accomplished something special for all catkind with him. Dad grew up as a "dog person" and never really had any exposure to cats. He had no dislike for cats. He spent his whole life, until he met Mom, as "cat neutral." Mom, on the other hand, has always been a "cat person" and loves all catkind.

When he met Mom she already had a cat, Kirin, a lovely calico girl. Kirin was like a daughter to Mom and had been with her since Mom was a teenager, and they were understandably close.

Although Dad and Kirin spent a few years together, he remained "cat neutral." After all, Kirin was clearly her cat and there was some fighting between them for Mom's attention. Dad and Kirin had an amicable, if distant relationship.

Skip ahead to the moment in the car, when Mom pulled off the box to reveal cute little me under it. Dad always says that's the moment he officially became a "cat person."

To reward him for embracing catkind, I've always made sure to show my love for him. I also make sure he sees my respect for him by following his rules (at least when he's there to observe it). From the start he tended to be stricter with the rules of the house, while Mom let me walk all over her (literally and figuratively).

When he says to stop something, I stop whatever I'm doing, politely and respectively. When she says "No" it's interpreted as – optional. I'm willing to take her "No" under advisement – sometimes I'll stop and sometimes, not so much. When I won't stop, she'll ask him to tell me "No" at which time I stop – the large majority of the time.

Dad isn't much of a snuggler so it's always been challenging to show my love for him. When he sits still for any stretch of time, I'll stand right next to him and mewl until he scoops me into his arms (it's best not to startle him by jumping right on him. He can be a bit skittish). Eventually he'll grow tired of my pleas, and he'll pick me up and arrange me in a position that works best for him. As a kitten I could be tucked in anywhere very easily but it's become harder as I've grown.

On really great days I'm given full lap access, but typically I'm given the place of honor right next to Dad. Sometimes he even falls asleep with me tucked under his arm.

I usually try to fit myself in the most unobtrusive spot next to Dad, and if it means that a third of my body must dangle off the bed or the couch, I'm fine with it. I will respectfully request some pets and enjoy each one.

He gives a nice rough pet and even when he goes against the grain of the fur it's still the best, and I enjoy every moment. We both love this special time together.

In contrast, I'm all over Mom when it comes to snugs. I like to take over the entire lap area. I like to be on her, rather than just beside her. I don't like to hurt Dad's feelings though, so I don't like him to see us together, don't want him to be jealous. As soon as the back door opens I jump right off, guiltily, as if it never happened.

I'll admit when it's cold in the house I'm often slow to jump off, because she's so nice and warm. Sometimes Dad can be quite stealth-like and when I don't hear him coming, he can catch us together. He's fine with it.

"He sees you snuggling with me, little cat." Mom will say smugly.

When they fight over who'll get to snuggle with me, by both calling my name and cooing, I always pick Dad.

"This is my kitty!" He'll say as he snuggles me close to his heart. If I could stick out my tongue at Mom in these moments, I sure would.

Mom calls me "Daddy's Girl" or "Your Cat" and frankly, I'm fine with both names. Dad loves me so much he even volunteered to own the litter box chores – now that's love. I was settling into the role as official "Daddy's Girl" when I learned I wasn't the only Daddy's Girl.

I was not an only child.

I'd smelled dog in the house and even heard one outside from time to time. She'd often bark at any intruders. On occasion, standing on the tippy toes of my back paws, I could even catch a glimpse of a blur of fur through the window of the back door.

I'd sometimes get locked up in our bedroom for no apparent reason. During my confinement I'd see large paws under the door. No, I was not alone.

"Do you think it's safe to introduce them?" Mom asked from the other side of the bedroom door one day. The tension was clear in her voice as I imagined her hands wringing with worry. I sat on the other side of the door – waiting.

"I'll keep a hold of her collar the whole time," Dad said with firm authority.

"Koda could eat her in a bite!"

"Don't worry, Koda won't hurt her." Dad's voice was sure and steady. I could hear the rattle of a large metal leash. Could she really eat me in a bite?

"WOOF!"

I admit I was a bit scared then, because her bark was very loud, and her paws were very large. I thought about heading under the bed, but if Dad vouched for her – well, she must be okay.

I carefully reached my front paw out from under the door and patted the giant paw with mine in friendship. She leaned down and sniffed at me under the door. She began to excitedly dance with those big white paws.

"I got her, no one's gonna get hurt," Dad said with full authority. "Open it up."

I got my first real look at her then. Koda took my breath away. She was a beautiful blonde husky and she towered over me. She looked at me with her beautiful light blue eyes and I knew she would never harm me. She sat down and looked up at Dad with the same adoration that was on my face when I looked at him.

I felt a slight stirring of jealousy.

"It's okay Koda, you can say hello. This is your sister. This is Fin."

She was very careful as she gave me a thorough "Hello" sniff, and just when I thought the fun would begin, she was ready for a walk with Dad. She was like that at times, all business.

She was an excellent sister dog. She explained that Dad was the leader of the pack, she was second in command, and Mom was third. I explained that I really should be number two, but we agreed to disagree. There was never any chasing or unpleasantness of any kind between us.

I didn't bother her much either, except when I played with her tail (couldn't resist – it was so floofy – who among us could resist that?). She always pretended I wasn't playing with it. We really only had disagreements when she ate my kibble.

Koda was the best dog in the world, until we lost her a few years ago. She even let birds use her molted fur for their nests. We sometimes had to compete for Dad's attention, but when either of us lost out, there was always Mom to snuggle with.

I enjoyed having her as my dog. I still miss her. We all do.

FIXED BUT ALSO BROKEN

I'd been with my family for about six months when I "Went Into Heat." I'm not even sure what I wanted while "In Heat," but whatever it was, wanted it pretty bad. I'd roll on the floor and mewl all day and night – with no dignity.

"You're going to get fixed tomorrow," Dad said.

Frankly I was all for it, because whatever was wrong, I wanted it fixed too.

"Look Fin, we got you this cool carrier, wanna check it out?" Dad said.

"Meow," I said, agreeing with him on basic principle, plus it looked like it was a fun place to hang out. I loved a box and this one even had some look-out holes built right in. I was still mostly okay with it, even once the steel cage door was shut behind me.

I was even fine with the car ride, but when we arrived at "The Vet," I got an uneasy feeling in the pit of my stomach. Perhaps I'd agreed to getting "fixed" too soon.

I hated the smell of the place, all those animals and the harsh antiseptic smell that burned. I started to panic until I saw another cat in a carrier next to me.

"Hey psst, are you getting fixed too?" I called out to the white lady cat in the carrier. I idly wondered if that would be how Snow would look in few years. I wondered if Snow would have to be fixed too. Certainly Archie could use some fixing.

"No sweetie, not this trip. I was fixed a long time ago." She said (Oh My Cod, there were more trips than one?). "Don't be too scared. You'll be fine, but you're figure is never gonna be the same." Turns out she was right about that.

The next thing I knew I was taken into a room and was poked and prodded by a strange woman. Although my parents did their best to keep me calm, I didn't care for it at all. I certainly didn't care for The Vet himself.

"What do we have here?" He asked as he swaggered into the office. What kind of a crackpot VET didn't even know I was a kitten? More poking and prodding commenced.

I was ready to go back home, but to my horror I was left behind instead of leaving with my parents. Surely this was an error of some kind and I began to vocalize my protests to the staff of the establishment, to no avail.

The little cage I was shoved into was so scary with its steel bars. The smell of alcohol made me sick to my stomach. I wanted out.

Housecat Confidential

The next thing I remembered was waking up in discomfort in my belly region. When I tried to meow for Mom, I noticed my meow sounded quite odd and not like me at all.

I started to panic when my parents didn't come right over, and when I realized I was still at The Vet, my panic really began to escalate. When The Vet's staff approached, I became like a feral animal, and growled with the fierceness of a lion.

The Vet was so concerned by my distress, that I overheard him call Mom and told her to come down right away. When she arrived, she was whisked back to the cage area. She heard a hysterical growling from the last cage, and she thought I must be scared by that wailing cry. Mom says she was scared too.

She looked in each cage as she passed by, expecting to see me, and was completely shocked when she got to the last cage with the hysterical growl, and it was me.

My eyes were so dilated I didn't even see who was reaching for me. It wasn't until I heard the sounds of her sweet voice, and smelled her scent that I was able to calm down and stop growling.

"Maow" I said crawling into her arms and hiding my head in her chest. I purred with all I had, which cut off any sound of the Vet.

She tried to assure me everything was going to be all right on the car ride home, but I was inconsolable. As soon as the cat carrier door opened I raced under the bed and remained there for hours. Mom even brought food and water under the bed, and tried to crawl under there to comfort me.

After the initial trauma wore off, and another trip to remove stitches was behind me, I began to live life again. We all noticed that my meow was different.

At first Mom just thought it was because of all the crying and growling at The Vet, but after a few weeks she realized it couldn't just be hoarseness. My voice had a lower quality and sounded a bit flat. I was fine in every other way but my voice seemed different, maybe because I was older and wiser. I had learned that I was not ever going into that carrier ever again willingly.

"Could you have broken my cat's meow?" Mom asked when she called The Vet. "She sounds different, kinda hoarse…"

"When she was under, something could have damaged her vocal cords."

He told Mom that she could bring me back so he could take a look. He also mentioned I might need another surgery if he was to try to repair any possible damage, and that any surgery might cause more damage.

Well there was no way I was going back voluntarily, and was willing to do whatever it took to not go back. I made that very clear to my parents, besides it wasn't hurting me in any way, so we decided to leave it alone.

I've had a slightly broken meow ever since. Instead of the full throated, inflection filled "meow" all cats have at their disposal to communicate, my new "meow" sounded a bit toneless to me. So I became creative and changed my vocabulary in order to find new ways of expressing myself.

I began to embrace my new voice, to think of it as a blessing. My parents found my new variations on "meow" so cute, they'd try to repeat the sounds back to me. We've managed to communicate very well as a result, it's even aided Mom in writing this book. Although both of them enjoy conversing with me, Mom seems to understand my words and body language better than anyone else. She often acts as my interpreter.

You may find that some of these variations are also used by your cat. They may still be recognizable to you or your feline charges.

- "Maow" – Means, "I like what you are doing here - with the petting. There's no need for you to stop, please continue." This is typically extended with half-closed, dreamy eyes and a gentle kneading gesture with the front paws, on any soft tender area of the human body available. It's the equivalent of "Meow."

- "Merr" – Means, "Hello" or it can be used as a greeting of pleasantries when all is right in my world. It can be said softly or in a medium tone. It's typically extended with a happy tail swish when seated, or a straight tail held aloft when standing. It's also the equivalent of "Meow."

- "Mah" – Means, "I'm a bit displeased." Perhaps my dish is less than full or perhaps the pets I'm receiving are mussing my fur. It indicates a course correction is required, but still in good spirits over all. It's typically extended with a very slight flattening of the ears and a glare of the eyes.

- "Mmmuh" – Means, I'm highly irritated by the lack of attention to my needs, and don't have it in me to even open my mouth to discuss it. This is issued as a humming sound, typically from a lying position with most of the body turned away in disdain. A deep sigh can also be added at the end for additional effect.

- "Merr-Oww" – Means, "I'm lonesome and would like some attention now." This is typically wailed in the hallway when searching for my parents. This call is begun with short syllables, heavy on the "Merr" but if they don't respond then I'll extend the syllables, heavy on the "Oww" and it gets much louder. This is very similar to the sounds normal cats make when they go into heat and want something. They combine it with their back ends up toward the sky – my version doesn't include that gesture.

- "Ra-oww" – Means, "Where are you? Why aren't you where you should be?" This can range in intensity from mild questioning to all out yowling, and is typically used in conjunction with "Merr-Oww."

- "Mew" or "Mew!" – Means, "It's fairly urgent things are taken care of now," for example dishes are actually empty. The sense of urgency is conveyed in the inflection and in the loudness with which it's extended. It can come out quite cross when it's ignored. The accompanying body language is very tense with tail held in a straight firm line, like a furry exclamation point.

- "Mew?" Is used when there's a question regarding something of an urgent nature that displeases me; for example to inquire why a wet towel has been left in my sink bed. It's extended with the tail held aloft with a slight curve, like a question mark.

- "Ka Ka Ka Ka Ka" – Is used when there's a bird or bug being stalked. It's given in order to lull the prey into a state of peace. It's typically accompanied with a wiggle of the hindquarters that indicates I'm preparing to pounce.

- "Eh Eh Eh" – Means, "Dad you're squeezing too firmly – I'm not a squeak toy. Please take it easy with the goods." At which time Mom will usually ask him what he's doing to "Her Cat."

- "Naow" – This can mean many things, and it's used as a fall-back when even I am not sure what the issue is. Here's an example of how it's used in daily conversation.

    "Naow" (Something is not right in my world)

    "What's wrong?" Mom asks.

    "Naow?" (I don't know, but let's find out together shall we?)

    "Do you need food?"

"Naow" (I'm not sure, let's take a look. I'll walk very slowly in front of you)

"Cat, move out of the way, or I'll step on you! Look, you have food."

"Naow" (It couldn't hurt to add some more, you know it's best when it's to the brim)

"You're not getting any more. I already filled it today."

"Naow" (Okay that wasn't it anyway)

"What is it Timmy? Did Lassie fall down the well?"

"Naow?" (Really, what does that even mean? Your humor can be so elusive)

What do you want? Does your litter box need to be cleaned?"

"Naow" (No. Do you want to look anyway? You can follow slowly behind me again)

"Do you want to snuggle?"

"Naow" (Maybe, but I can't admit that. Try scooping me up and let's see how it feels)

"Well come over here and I'll pick you up. Are you going to make me come over there?"

"Naow" (Yep)

"Naow" (Nope, that wasn't it either. Put me down now.)

This can go on for quite some time, until, in frustration, Mom stops replying. Then after a few more cries, I'll move into a couple of silent ones until I give up. I need a nap by now. All this communicating is exhausting.

- "Meh, eh, eh, eh, eh" – Means, "I'm doing something a little scary and if I'm in any danger please stop me, if not please let me do it." It is issued in a high pitch to indicate nervousness, the scarier the activity the higher the pitch.

- "Errr" – Is issued as a short growl and means, "Warning, you better knock it off or you'll regret it soon." If you miss this communication, and the accompanying flattening of the ears, you may be getting a little bitey soon.

- "Rrrr-Ahh-Oww" – Means, "I'm over-stimulated now and you're about to be attacked with some force. I'm sorry about that, but you should have paid attention when I said "Err." Don't blame me; it's your own fault."

I find many things can be expressed with little or no words.

- A slight tilt of the head with sad eyes and a paw hovering over the lap means, "You're kidding right? I'm not actually being denied access?" I'll remain in this position until granted lap access or until shushed away, at which time an indignant "Mah!" will be issued.

- A slight raise of one eyelid, after you've said "No" indicates I'm calculating your distance and wondering how much damage can be done before you'll get up and chase me off.

- When I crouch close to the floor and run very fast, using only the paw toes, it means, "I'm scared and need to hide right now. Please come find me in a few minutes, and assure me everything is okay. I'll be waiting under the bed." This usually happens after the doorbell is rung.

- When I suddenly jump up and grip the doorframe with my front paws and slide down it with a saucy look it means, "Let's Play! I'm gonna take you down, Momma. Please chase, but don't catch me. Just make a good show of it."

- A mincing dance with slightly crossed back legs means, "My litter box needs to be cleaned immediately or there's going to be a real situation here. Please get right on it."

- When you call, and I look away with an upturned nose, it means, "No. I'm not getting up to come over there (you know I don't come on command!), and don't come over here either; I'm in no mood for attention now. I'll come find you when it works for me, 3:00 am this morning sounds good. See you then."

- A paw gently petting your face means, "I love you very much and would like the gesture repeated on me. Thank you for understanding."

Although if it's a solid whap it could mean, "I'm really angry, let's fight it out."

- A cold shoulder turned your way, delivered in a sitting position, coupled with a refusal to speak means, "I'm still cross with you for leaving me alone. I'll forgive you in a while but right now I don't like you – please don't do it again – really, please don't!"

- A combination of "Merr-Oww" and "Ra-oww" called out while Mousey is in my mouth is what Mom calls my "Strangled Cry." It's what I call my love song for my dearest, my Mousey.

Fin & Hart

MOUSEY AND ME –
A TALE OF FORBIDDEN LOVE

I couldn't go any further without talking about the love of my life. I spent so much time and energy trying to hide our love, but once I decided to write this book I knew it all had to come out, I had to tell it all. I can no longer keep my love a secret.

I know Mousekind is supposed to be my enemy, and therefore our love is forbidden, but I can't bear to keep quiet a moment more. I no longer care about what others might think of our love. The possible judgment of others will not stop me from declaring my love for you, Mousey.

Horrifyingly, I understand I'm even meant to kill and – gulp – eat your kind. Oh the horror – the felinemanity. Why would anyone eat a mouse when there's perfectly delightful cat food to enjoy?

I remember so clearly the day Mom brought Mousey home. I'm sure Mousey realized it was hardly love at first sight for me.

"Hey look what I got for you, Finny," Mom said as she ripped Mousey out of his packaging and threw him on the kitchen floor.

Mousey landed so close to where I was enjoying my nap, that he startled me. As a result I didn't approach Mousey for a number of days (okay, it was weeks).

Mom isn't particularly diligent about sweeping under the dining table in the kitchen, so Mousey remained untouched for some time. I could see, even from a distance that he was a real looker, but I can be skittish about new things.

When Mom finally swept Mousey out from under the table, she threw him into the living room to get him out of her way. Mousey sailed across the room with such grace and distinction. I was mesmerized watching his long, grey, faux-fur tail wave in the breeze saucily.

"Jingle, jingle…" Mousey's internal bell made me long to toss him in the air myself.

I knew then that we were meant to be together, but I didn't want to appear to be too easily won over by his charms. I played it cool and waited for everyone to go to sleep that night.

Approaching his new resting spot in the living room, I got my first sniff of the catnip Mousey used to wear. It drove me crazy, and had to walk away or tip my paw with how I was feeling. I can be shy, and foolishly feared his rejection.

It was so hard to read his beady eyes at first.

Over the coming weeks he drew me in with those beaded black eyes, grey faux-fur coat and those adorable pink felt ears I longed to nibble. I remember fondly the first time I batted him gently and tentatively with my paw while everyone else was asleep.

"Jingle, jingle..." Mousey's tinkle ball called out and drew me in.

Mousey, you had me at jingle.

At first I wanted to keep our love a secret, waiting each morning for everyone to leave the house before we'd play together. I'd toss him in the air while he'd jingle, and take him with me to all my favorite nap spots, so we could snuggle the day away together. I had both my parents fooled, thinking I didn't care for Mousey. I never let them see us together, but they became suspicious eventually.

"Hey, did you move that mouse?" Mom asked.

"No."

"I keep finding it all over the house, but Fin never plays with it. I thought it was you tossing it out of the way."

"No, I thought you were moving it. Guess she is playing with it."

"Fin, are you playing with the little mouse?"

I just stared back at them as if I didn't understand, although my heart was pounding. Our love remained a secret for some time – until the morning we were discovered.

I honestly thought Mom had left the house. I was carrying Mousey in my mouth and singing to him. He was jingling along in that way he has. I rounded the corner and didn't see Mom sitting there, until it was too late, and she saw us together.

Of course I dropped Mousey, mid meow, and pretended it never happened, but I saw in her eyes that she knew the truth. I saw the look of shock, and then the gradual look of understanding and acceptance.

She understood that I'd found joy, regardless of the scandalous nature of our love, and accepted our relationship. After that I grew less careful about hiding our love. I remember how Mom once even found him in the big bed under the covers.

I try not to even think of the dark time when we were apart.

"FIN! I almost fell. I thought that stupid mouse was you!" Dad yelled.

I'd left Mousey in the middle of the hallway by mistake and Dad had tripped over him again. Dad became cross, and locked Mousey up in the hallway cabinet.

"No mice until you stop leaving them in the hallway!" He said shaking his finger in a punishing way. Unfortunately Dad forgot he put Mousey in there.

I know Mousey could hear me through the walls of his oak prison, I cried at the cabinet door for days for Mom to rescue him, but she didn't know Mousey was in there. When she finally noticed Mousey was missing, instead of questioning Dad, she just bought me another mouse toy, as if any mouse would do.

I don't need to tell you how much I disliked "The Other."

Thank goodness Mousey never had to see it. It was white with a black stripe, like some kind of a reverse skunk, and it reeked heavily of the nip. I tried to drown it in my water bowl.

"Oh Fin, you dropped your mouse in your water bowl," Mom said as she fished The Other from the bowl and left him out to dry. "How cute, were you giving it a bath?"

It lay on the tile, its white fur matted and mocking. I couldn't hold back my hatred, dropping it in the water bowl two additional times before Mom finally realized it was no accident.

I could hardly believe it when she brought home yet another imitator to take Mousey's place, as if anything could.

I picked up that new mouse, walked right into the hallway bathroom, and right in front of Mom, dropped it in the very tall water bowl my parents sit on.

"Are you trying to drown it?" Mom saw the look in my eyes and finally realized that I was a one-mouse cat and set about finding my love. It took much fruitless searching under all the furniture, before she finally understood my hallway cries and found him in his dark cabinet prison.

Now that he's back, I keep him safe at all costs. I keep him out of the pathways of my parents, for fear they'll step on him, and even risk an encounter with our arch enemy, "The Dyson," to rescue him from its path.

Now that our love is finally out in the open I can carry my love proudly in my mouth, singing out my song of love. I still don't like us to be seen together by anyone, but it's okay if they hear us.

Mom says my song sounds like I'm chocking, but Mousey is plump, and it's hard to enunciate with him in my mouth. I can tell by his soft jingle that he enjoys my song as much as I enjoy singing it.

I won't let you go again, Mousey.

Housecat Confidential

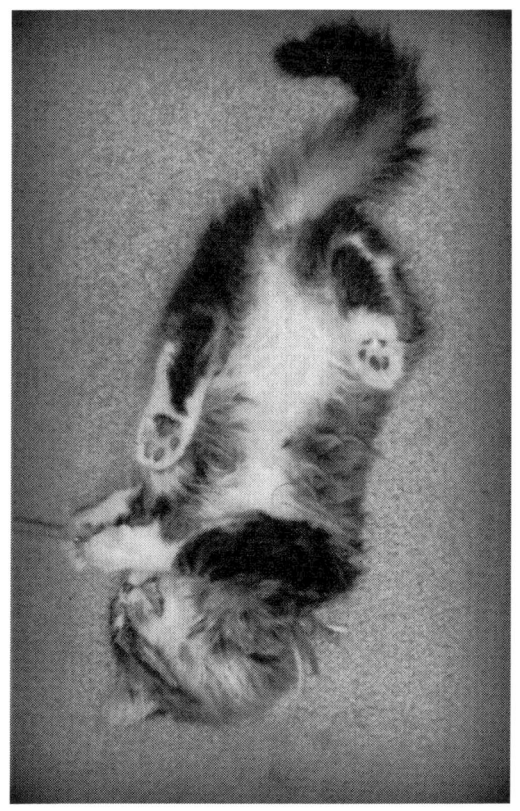

Take that!

Fin & Hart

THE SECRET OF LIFE – TAKE TWO

Okay I think I remembered it again. Hey, why don't I curl up here in the sink and you can pet me while we talk?

Oh that's nice... purrrr… yes, right under the chin… Mmm… Zzzzzzz

Fin & Hart

Housecat Confidential

Pounce in... three... two... one!

Fin & Hart

LET THE GAMES BEGIN

"No! Get down!"

"No! No! Get Off!"

"Fin, knock it off!"

"No, don't eat that!" were the daily choruses in the house during my kitten years. Any cat will tell you that we enjoy playtime almost as much as a good nap, and I'm no exception. Nothing's as frisky as a kitten. I was all play in my youth.

Of course my playtime activities have changed a bit as I've grown older. Playtime involves less physical activity than it once did. There's a delicate balance between staying fit and overdoing it and I don't want to visit The Vet again, if it can be avoided.

As a kitten, anything and everything was my cat toy – anything from the ladder Dad brought in to paint the living room (It was so fun to run up the rungs and see things from such heights), to the brushes he used to paint it. My parents realized that for all of us to stay happy, and for me to stay out of trouble, they needed to focus my youthful exuberance on proper pastimes.

"Look Finny, I found an exact copy of the toy we played with at the shelter!" Mom exclaimed as she swished the toy around the floor.

I was overcome by two things; my desire to pounce, and missing my fur family. My desire to pounce on the long string which split into a number of short strings at the bottom quickly won out.

"Swing it up high!" Dad would yell so I was able to leap for it and show off my acrobatic abilities.

"Ahhhh!" They'd exclaim as I'd leap high in the air, twisting my body in great arcs, often completing a full turn while aloft.

Nowadays, a floor chase is recommended; sadly no grand leaping arcs.

My parents used to buy those very small toy mice (you've seen them; they're covered in real fur and sometimes filled with catnip). I'd throw them in the air and bat them furiously on the floor – they were great fun, for about ten minutes – until they'd land under a piece of furniture, where they couldn't be reached anymore, and the fun was over.

My parents don't buy them anymore as my "mouse habit" was getting very expensive. Is it ever going to be fun when my parents finally move the sofa in the great room. There might even be an hour's worth of fun – until they're moved under another piece of furniture. It's like a layaway plan.

Dot on the other hand is very mysterious; she's small but her heart glows red.

I look for Dot sometimes when I want to play. I can never seem to find her when I look, but every once in awhile, always when my parents are home, she suddenly appears out of nowhere with attitude to spare.

Dot races across the floor, sometimes even across the furniture, with reckless abandon. She'll just hover on the floor waiting for me, but then she can also run up the walls where she can't be followed. At some moments, it seems Dot could almost be caught, but no – she's so elusive. It's okay though, since it's not very satisfying to catch Dot anyway. She seems to be totally without substance.

As an indoor cat there isn't much of an opportunity to stalk things. Stalking is a favorite feline pastime, so I've had to become very creative with stalking on "The Inside." Movement is critical and since there aren't many things to choose from, I stalk Mom.

She's rather slow moving, so chasing her isn't real challenging. Let's face it, even a hard bite to the ankle isn't likely to bring her down (tried it plenty of times and it just gets me in trouble).

I like to lay in wait for her to pass by, under the dining table or in the hall bath. When she finally walks past, I race out directly in front of her path, often banging right into her calf which startles her.

"Ah, you little stinker!" She says, accompanied by a little yelp, bonus for me.

"Mew!" I say racing to the nearest door frame. I leap up, grab it with my front paws and slide down, into a coiled position, and ready to strike. I like to put on my most mischievous look and challenge her with my eyes.

"You think you can take me, little cat?" She'll ask when she's in a playful mood, her eyebrow rising as she crouches down a bit.

"Mew!" Yes, sure do!

"Let's do this thing then!" She chases me around the house for a few minutes.

Luckily we have both gotten older and out of shape at about the same rate so we generally tire at the same time. I really hate it when she actually catches me though.

"Not so tough are you, Tinkerfluff cat?" She says as she scoops me up and belly snorgles me. It's so humiliating.

Of course when the weather is nice I spend hours on the porch stalking the birds, but sometimes my other prey finds a way inside.

I am the Mighty Bug Huntress! My bug hunting prowess is known throughout the land (well, at least I hope it will be now).

No bug makes it into my realm without my knowledge (except maybe ants, but who cares about them?). Land rovers are immediately killed with a hard blow by my paws of doom, a one-two punch, after being toyed with for awhile.

"Kill it! Kill it!" Mom will scream as she begs me to finish them off from a nearby perch (sometimes, I let them live, just to mess with her).

Sometimes I just look at her real intently and then point at her with my paw just to freak her out.

"What? Oh My Cod, is there a bug on me!" Mom will screech as she shakes her hands through her hair hysterically.

Oh, I slay myself!

The flyers require special assistance from Dad, as we hunt together.

"Ka Ka Ka Ka Ka" I'll call out racing over the floor or furniture alerting my parents to the potential peril they're in.

"Finny has a moth!" Dad says as he leaps from the couch and races to find a rubber band or a swatter, so we can begin the hunt in earnest.

His aim is legendary with a rubber band, but occasionally he misses and they fly away – so we search together for the intruder. When he finally brings it down to the floor I finish it off with my paws of doom.

In my younger years I felt obligated to dispose of the beast's carcass by eating it, but nowadays my work is done once I've landed the death blow. No one likes the taste of moth anyway; it tends to repeat on you.

I like it when my parents stay in bed late on a Sunday morning because the Blanket Monster comes out to play. The Blanket Monster isn't really as scary as it sounds, so don't be too frightened. The Blanket Monster was initially borne out of an innocent misunderstanding on my part as a kitten.

I was under the bed covers one night getting busy with some back leg bunny-kicking on a pillow when there was this odd trumpeting noise.

"Tooot, Tooot – Toot"

What was that, I wondered, continuing my pillow killing.

"Roooaaarrrr" A large beast's rumbling growl came from Dad's side of the bed. I was so scared; would the beast hurt him, would it eat me?

I prepared for battle, as the putrid smell of its fowl breath swirled all around me. When another louder growl came, I ran out from under the covers to escape. I was still only a kitten, after all.

My parents laughed and assured me it was nothing to be afraid of – it wasn't a monster after all – just farts – which can be quite scary.

After the first terrifying encounter they liked to tease me with the threat of the Blanket Monster returning.

Nowadays the Blanket Monster is often my parents wrapping their hands in the blanket and attacking me.

Due to the protection of the blanket I'm allowed to attack with total abandon. I can bite, land vicious bunny-kicks with my back paws, and act like a real killer kitty. Luckily my parents aren't harmed – much. Boy, it's a good time.

A couple of words of warning on the Blanket Monster game, should you try it at home. Be very careful that it is playtime and not just the movement of your mother's foot in her sleep (been banished to the hallway for that mistake). You can get yourself pretty worked up and think it's okay to continue the fighting, even when they take their hands out from under the blanket. It's not okay.

I also like to chase the birds in my yard too. I'm able to do this even from inside the house, because their shadows show up on the draperies in the living room. I can see the shadows as they fly through the air and move from tree limb to tree limb. The yard birds aren't satisfying to catch. I just end up with a mouth full of cotton drapes, when what I really long for is their feathery goodness. The yard birds are much more fun to stalk when I go outside.

Ever notice how most things are better outside, every experience is heightened. I'll sniff something outside and my parents will say how cute it is, while I sniff things in the house all day long and it's rarely ever mentioned.

I don't want you to think it's all fun and games, being a housecat is a great responsibility.

Is that a bird?

I'll get you my pretty!

MY LIFE'S WORK

Since the day I arrived, I've become a crucial member of my family, as I'm sure all kitties become. I was all play as a kitten, but over time I began to take my job as the family housecat very seriously. Now, I think of myself as a critical cog in my family's wheel of life.

In my position of housecat, I've assigned myself many duties to fulfill. It can be very challenging work. The life of a housecat can be quite stressful. It's a lot of responsibility on my furry shoulders, but it's very satisfying too. The rewards are great (well, they could be greater; my parents can be stingy with the treats).

There are so many things to do around here but waking Mom is something I consider my life's work. In part it's very challenging because I can't tell time. I'm a cat after all, and cats really don't appreciate the constraints of time. There's no time clock for us to punch.

As a result I try to go by the rising of the sun to get a handle on the appropriate time, but this has proven to be a problem; apparently this changes throughout the year (who knew?). So I go by when I think the sun should rise, or when my dish is empty, or when water is not fresh.

On most days the wake up call begins by climbing onto Mom's hip or on her tummy. She's pleasantly plump and it's a challenge to climb her. I guess I could just walk the long way, around her feet, to her face, but where's the joy and excitement in that?

"Fin! Get your paws of steel off of my (insert tender body part name here), you're killing me here!"

This usually wakes her, but sometimes she'll pretend it doesn't. She'll fake being asleep, but I'm not easily fooled. I've been at this for some time now, so time to move onto phase two.

Phase Two involves meowing repeatedly, right in her face (with only an inch separating us), and with great emphasis (especially if dishes are empty). She often has the nerve to pretend to still be asleep. She'll pull the covers over her head and say things like "Shh." This doesn't stop me for long. I can meow for long periods when needed.

Phase Three involves reaching out and softly petting her face with my paw. This can be accomplished even if she's hiding under a sheet – may get an eyeball instead of a cheek, but that's her fault, not mine. She'll brush my paw away, but eventually she'll reach out and give me a pet in return.

Whenever she stops petting, I pet her face in order to get her jump started. I find this shared petting experience to be very satisfying, but eventually it's time to move on to the business at hand (cat food cans don't open themselves).

Mom getting out of bed is the official start of the day; it's not enough to just wake her. If I fail my mission, and she's awakened by the noisy box instead, the whole day is ruined. Without my perseverance she could fall right back to sleep, if left on her own.

When the sun is actually coming up, or when my bowls are empty, I put real intensity behind my efforts. I move into the creating chaos phase (to be honest, at this point I'm usually a bit miffed at being ignored).

I'll knock over anything on her nightstand that'll make a crash, and if something spills (like a water glass), it's a bonus. I'll paw at the shower door or bathroom cabinet. I'll crackle paper on the floor, or pull some papers from the trash if necessary; whatever it takes to make it impossible for her to sleep any longer. I have to be careful not to wake Dad though or risk getting scolded. It's a delicate balance and quite challenging.

Adding to the overall challenge is that at certain times of the year the time of the sunrise changes overnight, throwing me all off. It throws Mom off too.

"Are you fluffing kidding me, little cat? Do you know what time it is?"

"Mew." You know I can't tell time; doing my best here.

After a couple of days of innocently missed cues on my part, she becomes less trusting and less willing to arise at the first request. As a result I'm forced to turn to more drastic measures. Simply knocking things off the nightstand isn't going to cut it.

Over the years I've formed a plan which I'm happy to report is foolproof. The element of surprise is critical. If you can, distract your human now my kitty readers, and read this part later.

One night I was sitting on the bathroom floor, waiting for the sun, when I suddenly noticed – the Moon. Sometime in the night, Mom had kicked off her covers, exposing a large section of lily white tush that actually glowed in the moonlight.

I was mesmerized by it.

Of course I've touched the butt before, but perhaps it was the coolness of the tiles, and a desire for a water refill, that lead to my next thought – what if I touched the "celestial body" with my paw, my cold paw.

No, better yet, my cold, damp paw.

I gripped the cool porcelain of the toilet with my front paws, and waited until I was adequately chilled. Then stuck my paw in the water bowl and headed off for –

A Moon Landing.

I made a stealthy approach, hoping she wouldn't turn or change the cover arrangement. I sat down, lifted my paw, and suddenly, felt a bit guilty.

"Mew," I said in warning, giving her an opportunity to awaken at my first request (okay, I whispered it, but I did do it).

No response.

I laid my cold damp paw upon the Moon.

One small step for Fin, one giant leap for catkind.

Now kitties, here's where the potential for danger comes – you need to leap back, you're going to need to be at a safe distance.

Prepare your most innocent look; you're going to need to deny any intentional wrong doing.

You might want to cover your ears too, with the dry paw, of course.

Fin & Hart

Housecat Confidential

You **again!**

Fin & Hart

MY JOB DESCRIPTION

Title: Housecat

Name of Supervisor: Not Applicable

Salary Rate: Wet food, kibble and water on demand, treats on a bonus schedule

General Summary of Duties:

- Sleeping

- Food Moocher - I'm not often taken up on this, although I do try. It's a shame, since I see it as a win/win situation for everyone. I do insist when it comes to tuna, beef jerky, and oven roasted chicken – you can't be too careful.

- Under Bed Inspector - Inspected whenever someone comes to the house. I like to give it a good check while my parents are greeting the guests. Once my parents are okay with them, then I'll give them a quick inspection too, from a safe distance.

- Greeter - If the guests are worthy of my company, I'll allow them to bask in my presence, and offer a friendly gesture (with floofy belly exposure) to welcome them.

  When they're cat lovers (yes, we can tell), I like to hang way back until they call me over in those goofy tones to show they're willing to embarrass themselves to get my attention. I'll walk over and sit just out of reach, so they have to lean way over to get a little taste of my fur. If I really like them, I'll grace them with a little snuggle (never on the lap, I'm not that easy). Always leave them wanting more. Well, there was that one irresistible cable guy (think he washed his pants in nip). I made a real scene (rolling around at his feet). I finally had to be locked in our room. Note to the Cable Man: If you're reading this, you know where I live – please return soon.

  When they're not cat lovers (and yes, we can always tell), I feel it's my responsibility, to all feline kind, to sway them into embracing us. So I pull out all the stops – exposing my belly, wrapping myself around their feet, even trying to get in their laps – until locked in my room.

- Hair Depositor - I ensure any article of clothing leaving the house has at least one multicolored hair of mine, but the more the merrier. Difficult, because they've invested in a large stock of lint rollers, and the evil Dyson vacuum cleaner. The trick is to get the hair into an area they cannot readily see, and best yet, where they won't think to look. The back of the calf, or the behind, is best in this regard. If you can lie where they sit, and roll around to loosen the hair, then they'll sit right on your fur. You can also rub yourself around their legs right before they leave. They usually only check the front of the leg, not the critical back of the leg. It's not foolproof, but it's good for a last ditch effort. No outfit is complete without cat hair I always say.

- Guard Cat - I'm careful to get plenty of rest during the day to stay ever vigilant against nighttime intruders, like moths. If I feel there's any danger, I'll wake Mom and alert her, no matter how small the danger, or the time of night.

- Writing Assistant - Oddly enough there are times when Mom doesn't appreciate my help, and rudely kicks me off the lap. She says she's "in no mood for a cat." Can you imagine?

- Fight Referee - I hate acting as a referee when parents disagree, don't like to choose sides. So when they ask me who's right, I give a non-committal shrug. I'm like Switzerland. Isn't it close to Fin Land anyway?

- Comic - I like to make them laugh, doing dumb things in order to amuse them. As a result they don't think I'm the brightest star in the sky, but that's where they underestimate me.

Position Entails: F - Frequent, O - Occasional, S - Seldom, N - Not Applicable

(F) Pouncing & Stalking (F) Sitting or Laying (F) Napping - Balled or Sprawled

Mental Tasks:

(F) Communicate Orally

(F) Perform Calculations (I can be very calculating)

(S) Listen to Directions (I can sense your skepticism - I can listen to directions, I just don't choose to follow them very often)

Environmental Hazards: Dogs, Large Scary Bugs of Unknown Origin, Mocking Birds, and Dust Bunnies

No. I won't look.

A DAY IN THE LIFE

When I hear humans say the life of a housecat is easy and boring, I have to laugh. We're cats; of course our lives are exciting; certainly my life is very exciting.

I think a day in the life of a housecat is thrilling. It could even be a documentary, a movie, a musical, or maybe even a television series.

I can picture it now, like "24," but with a tail.

1:00AM - The Ball Menace

Fade In

Fin is seen in profile, lying in the dimly lit living room. Her head is resting on her front paws. She stares intently, and warily, at an object just out of camera view. Camera pulls out to reveal The Ball (a toy cage made of green plastic which holds a shiny, menacing bell at its dark and evil heart). It sits directly in front of our heroine.

Fin rolls onto her back as she pretends to ignore it. After a few moments she twists her head to look at The Ball as it mocks her with silent taunts. She flips suddenly to face The Ball. It doesn't back down. She reaches out gracefully with her paw and almost touches it, but suddenly she leaps up and saunters towards the mouth of the hallway.

Fin thoughtfully listens for the sounds of her sleeping parents (Cue sound effect of very loud snoring). She is pleased her family is safe. She looks at The Ball with disinterest, but as she turns her head back to the camera we see the glint of mayhem in her eyes. Fin saunters casually past The Ball and tucks quickly behind a cabinet.

Cut to The Ball in the foreground and Fin in the background.

Fin settles into a crouch and wiggles her hind quarters as she prepares for a vicious attack. She pounces in slow motion. The Ball is helpless as it's caught in her ferocious bite (cue sound effect of the screaming tinkle of its jingle bell).

Fin stops mid-kill as she turns towards her sleeping parents (Cue sound effect of their snoring disrupted). Fin drops The Ball and covers it with her paws to silence its evil screaming. Fin wiggles her upper body to disorient it and whaps it hardily.

The Ball rolls swiftly towards the hall and the sleeping parents beyond.

"Tinkle, tinkle, tinkle, tinkle!" The Ball calls out in a loud and menacing tone.

Fin races after The Ball as it rolls towards her family. She throws herself on it, just as it makes a final break for the bedroom. She whaps The Ball and it rolls in terror back to its living room lair.

Fin curls up in the hallway corner, still vigilant and wary of another attack. Her parents snore loudly; blissfully unaware of the danger they've been rescued from.

Fade Out

4:30AM - The Aria

Fade in

Our heroine, Fin, is seen sleeping at the foot of the big bed. She is sandwiched between two large shapes wrapped in blankets. Fin stretches sweetly as she wakes up from her nap. She moves to Mom's head and gently taps Mom on the face with her paw.

"What?!" Mom says crabbily, as she pushes sweet Fin away. "You can forget it. I am not getting up to feed you – and don't even start with that mewing business!"

Fin leaps down from the bed in slow mo, and moves to the doorway to the hallway. Fin is illuminated by the nightlights. The screen morphs with wavy lines to indicate a dream sequence is beginning.

The scene is transformed as the lovely Fin is shown on a stage under a spotlight.

"Mew, mew, mew, mew, meeew" Fin says as she warms up her vocal instrument.

"Oh for the love… here we go again!"

Fin is encouraged by the shout of glee from the audience. A white cape is thrown from the audience which lands on Fin's shoulders. Fin shrugs as the cape sweeps over her shoulders dramatically.

Fin sings her aria which includes many variations on meow including Mew, Merr and the very popular Ra-ow. The crowd claps loudly as Fin completes her operatic aria. The crowd begins to throw roses at her feet.

Fin clears her throat and begins her encore.

Cut to a pillow camera shot, as a small decorative pillow sails through the air towards our plucky heroine. We see Fin smartly avoid the pillow by stepping to the side.

The dream sequence ends as we see Fin standing in the hallway surrounded by socks, a pillow, and a small towel on her shoulders. Fin lies down under the towel with her head on a pillow as her eyes sparkle (with enhanced computer graphics)

Fade Out

5:20 AM - Awakenings

Fade In

We see two humans sleeping in the foreground. In the distance our heroine, Fin, is sitting in the hallway watching over her family.

Housecat Confidential

"Mew! Mew!" Excuse me but I'm hungry!

"Shut it, it's flippin five am and I'm not getting up yet!" Mom says as she buries her head in her pillow.

We see sweet, hungry Fin pacing back and forth in the hallway. A short montage runs, showing many cute poses to music (perhaps to the song "Anticipation"). A timer runs in the corner of the screen to show an inordinate amount of time has passed (perhaps as much as three minutes).

"Mew!" I'm starving now! I've not eaten since last night! LAST NIGHT!

Dad stirs and then quiets.

"Okay! I can't take it anymore, I'll feed you," Mom says as she rises from bed.

Fin dances in the hallway as Mom lumbers slowly down the hall. The lively heroine Fin races ahead. Mom tries to read each can of wet food moving the can closer, then farther, then closer, distaste on her face.

Our heroine mewls loudly and pitifully as she dances around Mom's feet. She is growing weak from starvation. Mom cracks up a can in slow motion (cue sound effect). Mom places the TINY can of food onto a plate and plops it on the floor.

"I hope you're happy now."

"Mew?" Well, if you could pop it into the microwave for maybe ten seconds, just to take the chill off that would be excellent. Thanks for asking.

Mom walks away in a huff. Our Heroine shrugs and gets down to business licking off the gravy.

Fade Out

6:00AM – Good Morning Sunshine

Fade In.

Two humans are still lying in bed. Fin is watching vigilantly from a curled position on a nearby chair. She is exhausted but she remains awake. She wearily stretches her floofy legs and jumps in slow motion to the bed (Mission Impossible theme plays). She lands safely as we return to regular motion, and carefully navigates climbing over Mom's hip to reach her face.

"Mew!" It's time to get up.

"Mmph," Mom grunts as Fin gently pets her face with her delicate paw. "I already fed you, now beat it."

Clever Fin, seeing Mom is hopeless, dashes over her head to the nightstand. She begins to push Mom's glasses towards the floor. Fin narrowly avoids Mom's backward flailing hands as she grabs her glasses and tucks them under her pillow.

Fin looks determined, as she begins to scoot the full glass of water towards the edge of the nightstand and the bed beyond.

"If you spill that water on me again Fin, I will go Carnival Freak Crazy," Mom says in a menacing tone.

Fin, with great bravery and determination, scoots the glass just a bit more. Mom flips herself over with surprising speed. Brave Fin stands her ground and points to the hated noisy box.

The wild eyed (and haired) Mom looks at the clock which now reads 6:05am. Her face is transformed into softness as she realizes the situation, and scoops Fin into her arms for a forced cuddle.

"I don't have to go to work early today sweetie. Let's snuggle."

Fin is placed between her two parents and is showered with pets and scratches.

Fade Out

5PM - A Love Story

Fade In

Fin sleeps on the big bed. She stretches sweetly as she realizes the time draws close. She takes a long and luxurious lick bath, making sure each fur is in its place. She leaps from the bed, lands soundly on the bedroom floor, and she takes a moment to re-adjust her fur.

Suddenly Fin realizes her bath has taken too long and hurriedly begins her preparations. She dashes to the kitchen and wolfs down any remnants of food in her dish. She runs to the living room and moves Mousey back under the table.

Fin realizes the placement is too perfect, and tries to adjust Mousey with her paws. Still not right, she picks Mousey up in her mouth and tosses him gently so he lands belly-up and casual-like. She is pleased with the results.

(Cue sound effect of car on the street and the garage door opener) Fin runs through the office towards the laundry room. She sits down and tries several poses in an effort to look welcoming, but not overly so. She stretches to limber up, and she also tries several lying down positions. Yes, belly-up feels just right. (Cue sound effect of a car pulling into the garage on the other side of the laundry room door. The lumbering sounds of a human woman approach the door).

"Merr-ow! Ra-oww Ra-oww!" Fin says as she excitedly rolls on her back exposing her soft tender underbelly.

The door opens to reveal Mom as she enters from the garage. Her face is transformed with love as she sees our leading lady.

"How is my perfect furry girl? I missed you today. Did you miss me?" Mom asks as she leans down and gives Fin chin scratches. She scoops Fin up in her arms.

Fin basks in the adoration (for a full 10 seconds).

"Mah," Fin says, indicating she would like to be set down now.

Housecat Confidential

Mom gently places Fin on the floor as she heads down the hall. Out of the corner of Fin's eye she sees that The Ball Menace has placed itself in Mom's path.

Fin races past Mom and attacks The Ball with a solid blow to its evil green plastic hull. The Ball rolls cowardly into the living room as Fin races behind to ensure its submission.

"Tinkle Tinkle Tinkle" The Ball says fearfully.

"You saved me, my sweet cat!" Mom says with awe.

Mom and Fin go into the kitchen together. Mom cracks open a can of food while our leading lady rubs against her legs. We hear loud purring. The screen edges pull in until they are surrounded by a black screen in a heart shape.

"THE END"

Fade Out

Don't you just love a happy ending? I need a tissue.

Fin & Hart

Could you use a little snack? I know I could.

That's better.

Fin & Hart

I'M NOT AS DUMB AS I LOOK

My parents have, at times, mistakenly believed I'm not the smartest cat in the world (although I got Mom to write this book for me, so who's the smart one, hmm?). I'm not of course, but like everyone, I've had my tinkerfluff moments, like when I've craftily played dumb to get what I want. I'm sure you've heard of those tinkerfluff jokes – they're like the human equivalent of a blonde joke.

You know what I love even better? Those purebred prince/princess jokes, the ones that poke fun at how spoiled we kitties can be.

"How many purebred princesses does it take to find a patch of sun?" Answer: "None, they just require their people to buy them a sun lamp."

Oh those purebred jokes just slay me, almost as much as those "You Might be an Alley Cat if…" jokes.

"You might be an alley cat if you think of the whole kitchen floor as your food dish." Or "You might be an alley cat if you only know of Pedigree as a kind of dog food." So funny, I could just go on and on.

One thing my parents might point to, for their reasoning as to why I might not be the sharpest claw on a paw, is the fact that I often lay in the pathways and refuse to move when they're coming right at me.

I'll admit it; I enjoy lying in the pathways and am not quick to move out of the way, if at all. I like to keep an eye on the comings and goings and find the hallway is quite good for that. Sure, I'm smaller, but it's my house too, so why shouldn't I have full access to nap anywhere? Well the reason why I shouldn't is that Dad will often trip over me in the dark.

"Move it, speed bump!" He'll yell falling against the wall to avoid crushing me. He can be so clumsy.

I think this makes my parents the dumb ones, since clearly they can see me in the dark. Really, I see them.

Another reason my parents think I'm not so bright is that I'll paw furiously on mirrors, or on the glass fireplace screen. They think it's because I'm trying to attack the "other" cat.

Of course I know it's my own reflection. I'm not pawing at my reflection to attack or pet myself as they think; I'm making my cat music. My parents have named my cat music "That Racket." It's a catchy title, isn't it?

"Is that you making That Racket?"

"Quit making That Racket in there, little cat!"

Housecat Confidential

I think they really like the song because sometimes they clap their hands loudly and make up their own lyrics.

"Hey, hey, hey, knock it off!"

"I'm coming over there if you don't cut that out, cat!"

They don't seem to be on-key or very good with the rhythm, but I sure do love them for trying.

I'll admit I can get so involved playing That Racket against a door that it'll shut from the pawing, effectively locking myself in a room for hours on end. I should probably pay attention to the direction the door swings before starting to paw in earnest, but really, who thinks of things like that when the rhythm takes them?

One of the other reasons my parents don't feel I'm too bright is because of my dining habits. When I was young they bought me one of those bowls that have an attached reservoir to hold additional food which rests above the bowl.

For the life of me, I couldn't figure out how to get the food to come down out of the darn reservoir and was getting really hungry. Every time I'd draw my parents' attention to the empty bowl they'd think everything was fine because the darn reservoir was still full. It was so frustrating. I'd stick my head as far up that reservoir as I could go (almost getting stuck) and still the kibble refused to budge and fill the dish.

Till the day I die, I say it was defective.

Fin & Hart

One day I was so hungry, and wanted to call some attention to my plight, that I started pawing the food bag beside my dish. Well apparently the vibration from the pawing caused the food to finally let lose in the reservoir and fall into the dish.

I was so excited – dinner at last!

From then on, whenever the dish became empty, I'd paw at the bag hoping for a repeat. Unfortunately it didn't work again, but I still tried it each time the dish became empty.

Now here's where my parents think I'm dumb and I say brilliant.

Of course, I realized pretty early on it was a one time chance that the food came down. However, it's an almost perfect record that one of them will get up to fill the dish, in order to get me to stop pawing the food bag – and if they're so smart, why don't they just move the food bag? Hmm, food for thought, isn't it? Ha, that's funny.

Eventually, they became frustrated enough to purchase a normal bowl, one without any stupid reservoir. In fact, as an extra benefit, Dad mistakenly bought a dog bowl which was even bigger than the old bowl.

See, clever like a fox.

Another example they'd point to is the "Water Bowl Incident."

Housecat Confidential

My dishes had always been in the kitchen, until a couple of years ago when my parents decided to get granite countertops in the kitchen and a granite hearth around the fireplace. They rightfully felt I'd be freaked out with strange construction men coming in and disturbing the kitchen area. They decided that during the week of construction they'd keep the bowls in our bathroom, and I'd be locked in the bedroom during the day.

I spent the week in the bedroom and was really enjoying having everything ready for a snack upon waking. In the middle of the night, I could stand by the dishes and mewl until they got up to fill it. When the water needed to be filled, it was right by a faucet. It was all very convenient. When the workers went away, my bowls were returned to the normal spot in the kitchen.

Here again is where my parents think I'm not bright but I'm actually very bright.

Weeks later I was still crying for food and water in the bathroom, despite the fact they'd been relocated to the kitchen. Eventually my parents became so frustrated; they added a second water bowl in the bathroom. To this day, I still mewl for food in the bathroom, rather than by my actual dishes in the kitchen. They think it's because I forgot where my dish is (really, as if) and think it should be in the bathroom. Well, they're half right – I do think my food bowl should be in the bathroom, but what I really want is an extra food dish in the bathroom.

I will continue my protest until another dish is added. So you see I'm not so dumb after all.

Fin & Hart

Housecat Confidential

**Hey, where are my fish?
I left them right in here...**

Fin & Hart

MAKING A DIFFERENCE

I have no doubt I'm making a difference in my family, but as I've grown older I've felt a yearning desire to try to make a difference in the world at large. I don't like to leave the house, so it's been challenging to see how one small cat can make a difference.

Some of the ways I've found to help were small, act locally and think globally is what they say. I found a way to help a cat in need, right in my own front yard.

Dad had to go out to work late one night, and before he left, he told me to keep Mom safe. I take my assigned duties very seriously so I was up late, keeping watch, when a car approached. Naturally I looked out the front window to verify it was Dad returning. I was very relieved to see his car (ready to hit the sheets by then) – until the headlights revealed an intruder.

Right there, in my own front yard, was the illuminated outline of a feline prowler. I was instantly ready to fight, my tail in full floofed glory.

"Hey! Hey You!" I yelled out and whapped the glass with my paw, "Out of my yard!"

Suddenly I saw the outline of a paw being raised in an unrecognizable gesture. "What the Fluff!?! Same to you Mother Fluffer!" (Sorry for the potty mouth but I was very upset).

Just when things couldn't get any more heated, Dad came out of the garage with my old food bowl, and laid it out for the intruder (with my own bowl! Dad, how could you?).

The cat came timidly into the light and I saw it was a little black mancat. I was shocked to see it reach up on Dad's leg for a chin scratch, and noticed it had an extra set of paw toes.

Apparently, what I thought was an inappropriate gesture was actually just the extra paw toes raised in a wave. I felt a little guilty at the previous outburst. After calming down, my parents sat me down to explain.

Apparently "Mittens" (Mom's name for the intruder – yes, she'd given him a name) is a neighborhood stray who sometimes hangs out in our front yard, and has done so for years. He drops by when he's hungry and my parents give him some of my kibble.

I was very upset, until Mom reminded me that Mother Tabby was once homeless. I felt ashamed then; if not for the good fortune of finding my human family, it could be me out in the yard.

Mom was right – I was being harsh.

So I've allowed Mittens to stay in the front yard with my blessings, as long as he stays out of my backyard. I've even allowed a bed to be placed on the side of the house for his shelter. Sometimes I even call out to Mittens when I see him through the windows to say hi.

Other worldlier issues were harder for me to address. I've heard of many animals needing new families because people are losing their homes. I'm not sure how you would go about losing a home, as they're quite large. I know when Dad loses his house keys he becomes a raving nut; I can't even imagine how upset he would be if he lost the whole house. So I've enlisting Mittens' help to wave my parents in, if they should look lost or confused.

All this talk of hard times can really bring a cat down. I wanted to lift others' spirits, so Mom and I discussed it, and after much campaigning on my part, Mom finally agreed to write this book.

Let me begin by saying I made every effort to try to write this book without a ghostwriter, but paws aren't made for keyboards (tail and belly don't work either). The results were an illegible mess – guess pages of HHHHMNKKOEKLJEI2 would be a bit tough to enjoy. Plus I was frequently scolded for playing/laying on the keyboard.

If I could've managed to type, the results might have been page after page of "fill my dish, fill my dish, fill my dish," and although that's real and honest, it also wouldn't be that enjoyable to read – at least not after the first couple of pages anyway.

I spent countless hours lying directly on the keyboard as Mom tried to type around or over me (even persevering when she would try to push me off). When she wrote on paper, I batted at her pen until spent – and when she edited our work, I either pawed at the monitor when something displeased me or gave the cold shoulder when it was read aloud. It's been exhausting frankly; I've even given up some naps to get my stories told, but I'm very pleased with the final results.

The collaboration on content hasn't always been easy, but in the end the collaboration has been good for both of us. It's brought us closer together and hopefully it will bring you closer to the felines in your life – a way to bridge the species divide and bring about understanding.

Eventually our collaboration extended to a blog. Reaching out to the world has opened my eyes, and I saw the world has its sadness but it's filled with wonder too, with people who offer to lend a hand when they could turn away, and my spirits were lifted.

LIFE'S LITTLE PLEASURES

Sometimes it's the little things that can bring you joy. So here, in no particular order, are a few of my favorite things that you might enjoy too:

- Spending time in the yard. I was very scared of the outdoors initially, but over the years I've become quite brave on the patio. I love seeing all the birds enjoying the large fountain. They come for a drink, or a bath, and it's great fun to pretend to chase them. I honestly have no idea what I'd do if I actually caught one.

- Store bought ice cubes. They're far superior to the ones from the icemaker when it comes to playing ice hockey. I'm not sure why, but as a real connoisseur on this topic, there's a night and day difference between the two. I love to bat the cubes around the dining table in the kitchen. Hold out for the good stuff, kitties.

- Cellophane. I love it so. The crinkle and crunch of it, it's just like heaven in my mouth. I don't recommend actually eating it though. It can cause some real gastric distress which is why I try to only nibble it when someone is around to stop me from swallowing it. It's part of the fun actually. Mom gets totally grossed out when she has to grab the cat slobbery cellophane from my mouth. One time, I found a hidden cat toy while it was still in its cellophane packaging. I played with the bag all night. The next morning Mom found the toy sack peppered with teeth marks but the toy was still inside. She thought I was trying to get the toy out, but no – just loved the bag. Once the toys were liberated – it was the Cellophane I wanted.

- The Dining Room Table. No one really dines there but my parents often drop purchases there and it's what I call my Cellophane Hunting Ground.

- Speaking of Bags - I love bags, all kinds. I get right in. I prefer the brown paper over the plastic, as it's sturdy and able to handle a lot of action. They also make a lot more noise which annoys others and that's always good. I feel quality control is so important on this matter; nothing but the best will do, so I check every bag that comes in the house.

- Boxes. When I was very small I used to love getting in a shoe box because Dad would drag it around the floor like a little race car. We would go so fast, and he would make fun racecar sounds. I'd feel the wind on my face and imagine we were on the speedway. I thought my shoe box racer days were over. I'm too big for a shoe box now, but when Mom bought some boots, I was back in the race again.

- Tuna. Is there anything tastier than tuna? Mom isn't a fan, which is fine, because there's all the more for Dad and me. As soon as I see him in the kitchen by the can opener my heart races, just in case it's going to involve tuna. I can't contain excited cries to convince him to hand it over. All thoughts of anything else leave my head.

- Oven Roasted Chicken. I can smell oven-roasted chicken from any corner of the house, and come running as if the world would end if I didn't get there immediately. I won't be denied. I make a real scene till I get the treat.

- Beef Jerky. Dried beef in a cellophane bag, come on!

- Wet Food. I almost missed out on this delight. My first experience was a Trout flavor. Although I tried to enjoy it, it was not to my taste. It wasn't to Mom's taste either; she opened it and gagged as if she had a hairball. She opened all the doors and windows, and made Dad take it outside like it was toxic waste (what a drama queen). Finally I convinced them to crack open another variety (with gravy) and it's true love. Everything needs gravy, in my humble opinion.

- A patch of sun. Finding a natural patch is difficult because most of the drapes are closed during the day, but I have ways around this. I can create my own sun patch by moving the living room drapes back with my paw. My favorite patch is in Mom's craft room and as an added bonus – I can play with her things.

- The granite fireplace hearth. It's so nice and cool when it's hot out.

- The bathroom faucet. I like the faucet turned very low and then I stick my face right in it and sip from the stream. I'll sometimes get my whole head wet in an attempt to find the right angle. When I have to shake it off, the water spots make a real mess on all of the bathroom mirrors – oops.

- The bathroom sink. I love my sink and it's all mine since my parents gave it up for my exclusive use. It's a great cat bed. There was a time when I put on a couple of extra pounds and couldn't get into it comfortably. I realized I needed to watch the weight. I can't lose the sink due to my largess.

- Honey soap or glycerin soap. Yum. We used to have a soap shaped like an angel's face and I've licked its face right off – sorry.

- Petromalt. I get so excited when I see it. Mom lets me lick it right out of the tube. I guess it helps with hairballs, but I'd eat it either way.

- Mom's things. Anything belonging to her is good to play with.

- The sound of the garage door. I love when my parents return home.

The Outsider

I'm on the outside, refusing to look in.

Fin & Hart

PET PEEVES

I'm a happy cat by and large, but like everyone I have my issues. One of the things that plague me as a long-haired cat is grooming issues. Although I love my fur and the distinctive look it gives, it can cause difficulties.

I can sometimes get "knotty" (not "naughty").

Sometimes, during my lick baths, I'll manage to get a clump of my undercoat all lumped up together in an impenetrable knot (usually on the belly but sometimes oddly enough on my neck?).

It's so frustrating – the more I try to remove it, the worse it gets, until finally there's an unsightly clump of fur hanging off of me. It's very humiliating and very uncomfortable too. I'm forced to call attention to the situation so a "knotectomy" can be performed to trim it out.

Another grooming faux paw is an alphalpha hair or worse yet, when they morph into an alphalpha cluster.

What's an alphalpha hair you might be asking? Well I'll tell you, but any long hair cats out there probably know exactly what I'm talking about already.

An alphalpha hair is usually created when someone pets against the grain (which is so irritating after spending hours to get everything just right) in combination with my efforts to lick it back into place. The two factors can cause a knot.

The matted hair then shoots out from beneath the topcoat of fur, calling attention to itself like a freakish beacon, an arrow of grooming humiliation.

I'm still unclear on why it's called an alphalpha hair but I think it has something to do with "Our Gang" – I guess "My Gang" would be Mom and Dad – but I'm still confused. The rest of my gang does not get alphalpha hairs (plenty of other hair emergencies though), and I'm not affiliated with any other gangs.

Mom hates an alphalpha hair, and a cluster of them drives her completely nuts. It would almost be worth creating them just to bug her, but truth be told I don't like them either (they ruin my sleek lines). To avoid them, I could leave when the petting starts to go against the grain, but since it's Dad doing the petting, I allow it, of course.

Here is where the classic struggle begins.

Mom and I want the alphalpha gone but we both hate having it removed. So, while it's riding high, snuggle time becomes a battle of wills.

There's hair pulling (mine), biting (me again), bloodshed (Mom's), crying (both of us, but mostly her), and hurt feelings (again, both of us).

In desperation for a happy home once again, Mom tries to sneak up on the hair with a pair of scissors. By this time I'm ready for a fight anytime she moves her hands towards the alphalpha area (and really just the sight of a pair of scissors in her hands, even on a good day, is enough to make me angry), so it's a dangerous time.

"If you just let me cut it out we can be done with all this unpleasantness!" She'll beg in desperation.

When I can no longer take it, I'll pretend I don't notice the scissors, and sit still long enough for her to perform the knotectomy (don't worry she never gets close to the skin).

To avoid these knotty issues from ever happening, Dad occasionally gives me a haircut. I don't need to tell you that no self-respecting cat is going to still for – well, sitting still. There have been many incidences when flurries of my flailing and his scissors have collided during these sessions and the results have been less than attractive.

My resulting coat looked like I'd met up with Edward Scissorhands. There were hunks of my fur cut at different angles and too many different levels to count. Whiskers were once trimmed during the fray, and I don't need to tell you how traumatic that is.

"Oh my!" Mom would involuntarily gasp when she would first see me. "Oh, you still look darling," she would say as she covered my ears and hissed at Dad "What the heck happened?"

"What? She looks cute."

I'd hide under the bed in embarrassment until it grew out.

The bad hair months seem to have ended now. Dad has really improved his cat grooming skills over the years. We have a good system worked out now. Mom holds me during the trim, and for the most part I've learned to sit still, sort of. When it's all said and done, I admit to liking a shorter cut and it's much cooler in the summer.

Other than grooming issues, I don't have too many real complaints, but here are a few of the things that displease me, in no particular order:

- The sound of the garage door opener. I hate it when my parents leave the house. What do they do out there anyway?

- The rocks in my yard. We live in a desert climate and we have what they call "Desert Landscaping" and what I call "A lot of very pointy uncomfortable rocks." It really curtails exploration of the yard and severely limits chasing of the yard birds. I can get a nice stalk going but when running to pounce I can only run as far as the edge of the patio. It's so humiliating.

- The Mocking Bird. Once the Mocking Bird saw I wasn't able to chase it past the patio, it began to actually mock me. It'll swoop down and taunt with its loud calls. I might even break my no kill policy if given the chance to taste its feathers.

- The Dyson Vacuum Cleaner. It's hard to express how much I hate and fear the Evil Dyson. First there's the way it moves, as if it just floats across the floor; sometimes it even seems like it's chasing me. Luckily my parents are always around when the Dyson comes out. My parents always hold its leash, but it's so thin – I don't like to take chances. Then there's the potential danger to Mousey. As soon as I hear the door to the Dyson's lair open, I grab Mousey and we hide in the closet till it's gone. Finally, I work very hard to leave fur all around the house and the Evil Dyson wipes that all out. Curses to you, Evil Dyson.

- The Fax Machine. It lives in Mom's office and often comes to life mid-nap. It's very loud and jarring. I attack and shred any paper it sends through its mouth, can't imagine why this bothers my parents – I'm protecting them.

- The Bathroom Scale. Frankly I have no real issue with it, but it seems to make Mom upset every morning, so I dislike it in solidarity. Curses to you too, scale.

- The Hairdryer. I don't like a hot wind in my face, who would?

- Hairballs. One minute you're enjoying life and the next minute you're hacking uncontrollably. I know my parents would prefer the expelled hairball would land on the tile, rather than the carpet, but I really don't have a choice. Okay, I've a choice and choose carpet. You can really dig the claws in, helping with expulsion.

- Being picked up. How I dislike being lifted without approval and any forced snuggling while up there is also unwelcome. I do like being lifted when it's my idea of course, to kill a bug or to inspect something that cannot be reached.

- Moving furniture or new furniture. It can be quite startling to wake up from a nice nap and find your whole world turned upside down. I've grown a bit more tolerant of this activity in later years. There was a time when I'd hide in the closet for days. I'd actually like it if they moved the couch – I'd get my mini mice back.

- The Pawparazzi - Ever since we decided to write the book it's been like having the pawparazzi right in my own home. I should have seen that this desire to capture my kitty essence on film could develop into a real problem. I should've suggested a stunt cat.

    At first, I was more than willing to sit for portraits. Maybe willing is a stretch, but didn't feel the need to hide under the bed to find some privacy, like now.

    I pretended not to notice as they fumbled about with slow trigger fingers trying to frame the shot. How long can a cat be expected to wait?

    The fact the camera flashes first and then waits a few seconds before capturing the shot doesn't help either.

Someone (no one seems willing to take responsibility) thought it might be a great idea to sneak up on me sleeping, gently arrange me into a cute pose, and then awaken me to get "the look" they wanted. Well, no one likes to be awakened from a nap by flash bulbs, this isn't Hollywood.

- The Infidel. See next chapter.

Fin & Hart

THE INFIDEL OR THE HUSKADOR INCIDENT

After my Koda dog passed away, Dad really missed her and he thought another dog would heal our hearts. Mom thought it was too soon, but they agreed that when the time did come they would get an adult dog from a shelter; they felt a puppy would be too hard to manage. They wanted to get another Husky or a Husky mix, since my dog was perfect.

I wasn't consulted at all, by the way.

I guess sadness makes you do things you agreed not to, because within weeks, Dad went to the animal shelter, alone, and fell into "puppy love" with a beige husky mix with blue eyes. He thought her eyes looked like Koda's and he thought she was very sweet and lovable.

"Guess what?" He asked on the phone from the shelter. "I've adopted our new dog!"

"WHAT!" Mom yelled. "I haven't even met her! How do you know she'll be good with cats?"

"Well I already signed all the forms… she is getting fixed in the morning and then I can pick her up." Dad gushed with enthusiasm, as if he never heard her concerns.

Technically Mom wasn't consulted either.

The blue eyes were where the similarities to My Dog ended. This dog was nothing like my Koda.

The first night she came home she was still groggy from "being fixed." She was very mellow, and I was able to give her a close inspection. I wasn't totally pleased with another dog, but at that point, I was still reserving my judgment.

"Woof," she said as she picked up my love, my Mousey, in her mouth.

Whatever was supposed to be "fixed" still seemed pretty darn broken to me.

"NO! Not Mousey!" Mom said rescuing Mousey from her jaws of death.

It was pretty much the end of my open mind – she was dead to me from then on.

The next day the drugs wore off and all bets were, officially, off too. Shayla, the name Mom gave to her, was what we cats like to call "A Chaser."

"No Shayla! Don't chase Fin!" One of my parents would yell as soon as she came in the house and spotted me.

Naturally she ignored them and would tear after me with bloodlust in her "pretty" blue eyes. Luckily my parents were there to prevent tooth to fur contact.

My parents are an optimistic pair and thought if they slowly introduced us, eventually Shayla would realize I wasn't a movable feast. They hoped she would learn to ignore me, like my Koda did.

Of course if consulted, and again I wasn't, I'd have told them that no "chaser" is going to ever give up "the chase."

My parents were quite concerned that in my advancing years, I wouldn't be able to run fast enough or be able to leap onto high places where Shayla couldn't reach me. I was happy I didn't have to run and jump for my life. However, let me assure you that when fifty pounds of fur and teeth are coming at you, you dig deep and find the power to run as fast or jump as high as needed.

Shayla didn't understand any commands or pleas that my parents would call out to her, so she was rightfully relegated to the yard most of the time. She was only allowed in the house when supervised by Dad. She didn't listen to Mom at all.

During these indoor visits I was locked up in our bedroom, like a prisoner in solitary confinement, as if I were the naughty one. Meanwhile, "The Infidel," as I called her, was allowed to invade my turf. She'd even eat my food, right from the dish – the nerve of her.

During her time indoors she'd destroy anything she could get teeth on. She'd even pee on the floor – no self respecting pet should pee on the floor. Not that I was offering my litter box for her use, because that would've been completely unacceptable, but really, come on.

When she was outside she'd completely destroy the yard. The plastic bunny I liked to sniff, chewed beyond recognition. The bird feeder, destroyed beyond repair. The chair I enjoyed sitting on with Dad, eaten, yes, eaten – de-stuffed and eaten.

She was also a digger.

I'd watch her digging at the plants with reckless abandon. She even pulled out the drip irrigation causing an unplanned, larger backyard fountain. She would routinely come up to the back door to ensure I saw her naughty efforts.

"No! What did you do, Shayla?" Mom would cry while Shayla would attempt an innocent face with mud caked on her snout. If it hadn't been so tragic it might have been funny.

Every night when Dad came home and found our yard destroyed, he was extremely displeased.

I'd spend the entire day looking out the window on the tippy toes of my back paws. I even broke the mini-blind on the back door, in order to keep tabs on the Infidel's indiscretions. As soon as I heard Dad's car pull into the garage, I'd run to the door of the laundry room and report the Infidel's activities.

I was so stressed, I was barely able to nap and eat.

Still, Dad persisted in keeping the Infidel. He even called in a dog expert to see what could be done to curb her naughty behavior. Most concerning to Dad was her constant jumping on Mom. The Infidel would almost push her over (and she's awfully big to push over).

The dog expert thought the Infidel was a mixed breed of a Labrador and a Husky which is when Mom started calling her "The Huskador." The expert thought she could be trained, so my parents tried their best to train her. I even tried to be supportive by observing, from a high vantage point, of course.

"Sit!" Dad would say with authority – nothing.

"Sit Shayla!" Mom would beg – nothing.

"Sit! Sit!" Dad would say – suddenly she listened, and sat.

A complete fluke I say, but suddenly out comes a treat which she gobbled down.

I could hardly believe my eyes. She was being rewarded! Naturally, I wanted in on the treat action, so when they commanded it, I'd sit too.

"Mah!" I'd say, trying to call attention to my successful efforts.

"Fin, knock off that mewling!"

No treat was provided to me. My days helping with the training initiative ended.

Fin & Hart

The final drama came one night when I was innocently enjoying dinner.

Dad opened the back door and The Infidel pushed past him to get inside. My bowl is pretty close to the back door so there wasn't much room for error. So when we looked into each others eyes I knew she meant business.

"Ruff, Ruff!" she said as she raced past Dad, hitting the back of his knees, causing him to loose his balance.

He fell to the floor, barely missing the TV stand with the back of his head.

"NO!" Dad screamed in fear as The Infidel continued right past him.

"Ruff, Ruff, Ruff!" she said as her jaws came closer to me.

I realized I was cornered.

She was mere inches from my head when Dad just barely got a grip on her collar. Her jaws were snapping at me and I felt her hot breath on my fur.

"MEG! HELP! SHAYLA IS GONNA EAT FIN!" Dad screamed in desperation as he tried to pull Shayla back. He had no real traction as he was still splayed on the floor. He couldn't let up on the leash even an inch as she was already pulling it with all her might.

"I'M COMING!" Mom screamed but she was in another room, and she isn't a real fast mover, so she was clearly not going to be of any immediate assistance.

I'm not sure if it was that I'd just had enough of being chased by The Infidel, or if it was because she'd hurt Dad, but I didn't run away this time.

This is My House and My Parents and no one messes with them.

I reached down to the depths of my angry kitty soul, and turned around to fully face The Infidel.

I went into "Fur Ninja" mode. I growled, hissed, clawed with everything I had, and bit many times.

Now, in my defense, I really thought it was the dog I was attacking.

Unfortunately it was Dad's arm (and somehow in the confusion, his foot too).

After the blood was cleaned, Mom insisted "The Huskador Incident" come to an end.

My parents realized we were not going to be a happy family after all. They were sad, but the shelter assured them they would find The Infidel a very nice family; one without cats, and plenty of people to keep her busy.

I think it was best for everyone.

At this time I'm still an only pet, although whenever Mom sees a cute kitten on television she asks Dad if we can have another cat. She tries to tell him I might enjoy a baby sister to keep me company. Luckily he says no, as he instinctively knows I don't want any interlopers.

I shudder to think of some little pipsqueak kitten following me around twenty-four/seven and the inevitable sharing of everything that I hold dear.

Oh the thought of some cat trying to claim Mousey, oh no, I think not – stay strong Dad, don't let her sway you.

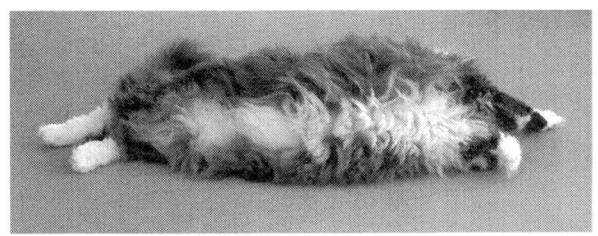

Who needs another pet, when you have all this?

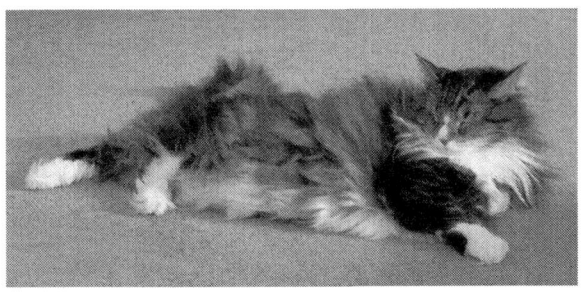

Fin & Hart

THE SECRET OF LIFE – TAKE THREE

Moth!

I'll get it!

Fin & Hart

HEALTH AND WELLNESS

I've been blessed with excellent health. Oh sure there've been the occasional hairballs that have taken me down for a short time, but by and large I've been able to avoid going to The Vet with any regularity. I cannot come close to expressing my deep distress over having to go to The Vet.

In order to avoid any need to return to The Vet, I have taken great pains to try to stay well. Here are my tips for living a healthy life:

- Get a lot of sleep. I think sleep is best in the form of long naps but any nap is a good nap.

- Stay away from danger. To accomplish this I primarily stay indoors (even when the door is left open). I don't stray, unless my parents are watching and able to protect me.

- Be a lover, not a fighter, unless you really can't avoid it. I had to fight The Infidel to protect my parents but other than that I go with a live and let live policy. Few things are worth going to war over.

- Get a good amount of fiber to avoid hairballs and to stay regular. Now this one is hard because there's not a lot of roughage to be had indoors. I've found that eating toilet paper (while it's still on the roll, of course; I'm not an animal – well you know), keeps you quite regular.

  In order to make the toilet paper go down easier, I like to lick the glycerin soap. I really like to lick the spout of the honey hand soap dispenser too (this also helps to get the taste of moth out of your mouth). I've been known to get scolded when caught (eating the toilet paper or the soap, actually).

- Keep on top of your daily bathing; everyone appreciates a clean kitty.

- Sit still when getting a haircut. Sharp shears close to body parts, it's kind of a no-brainer, but it did take awhile to learn it just the same.

- Keep fit. It's fine to be generous with your curves but be sure to keep yourself trim enough to fit in the places you love. Do the activities you love so it isn't such a bore. I recommend ice hockey and lots of toy action.

- Keep your bones strong by drinking lots of milk. This one is challenging since my parents don't like to give me milk. So I remedy this by sticking my face in Mom's glass whenever she pours one for herself and leaves it unattended for even a moment.

She doesn't like to share for some reason, so when she sees me do it she pours the remaining milk in a bowl, and I'm able to enjoy it without the threat of a spill. As a result, I try to have her see me stick my face in her glass, in order to get my own bowl, but I'm fine with sharing either way.

- Don't overeat. I know it can be tempting, when the bowl is overflowing, to gorge, but you just have to control yourself. Now, I'll admit to overeating when my parents go away for a few days (I'm a nervous eater). It's hard to be good when lonesome and bored, but in the end you're just hurting yourself.

- Stay engaged mentally. You need to keep the mental wheels turning up there. It can be monotonous being indoors and you need to find challenges to keep mentally spry. I like watching the History Channel or Animal Planet (who am I kidding? I love a cheesy reality show as much as the next cat). I enjoy making my cat music too.

- Always keep your sense of humor. I find my parents to be quite amusing. They're so cute when they expose their bellies, or scratch behind their ears. They're so precious when they're sleeping. They make me laugh all the time with their crazy human antics.

- Find a way to make a difference in world. No matter how small your world may be there are always ways you can add value and make the world better for your being in it. It can be easy to forget there are others less fortunate than you are when life is good. I never forget the stories Mother Tabby told me of her life on the streets. I'm always grateful for the life I've been given.

LOVE AND ACCEPTANCE

As you can imagine it isn't always easy for felines to live in the world of humans. Communication can be such a problem between us. Humans are typically so limited in their understanding of the feline language. "Meow" has so many meanings among cats; it's really all in the delivery.

Despite our differences, I've found all the love and acceptance a cat could want with my furless, two-legged family. I'm adored by my parents (I hear them coo about how adorable I am all the time), and I fully enjoy all the attention that's given.

I accept their love and give it in return. I know I'm safe in my home. I'm free to expose my soft tender underbelly when napping, knowing that no harm will come while my parents watch over me.

I'm forgiven for my transgressions: the occasional mess (okay, I make a lot of messes, but still forgiven), or the loud noises while playing in the middle of the night (I'm nocturnal after all). I'm rarely kicked out of bed for snoring (unlike Mom, I'll admit to snoring).

I'm showered with love and pets. I'm fed the finest cat food, it's often the diet kind, but still, it's not the generic (they buy premium brands). I'm given the best cat litter.

I forgive the transgressions of my family too. Some are easy to forgive, like the bad haircuts, the less than flattering nicknames (Chubbs and Speedbump), and the times I must remind them to fill my bowls with food or water. Some things are harder to forgive, like the trips to The Vet and The Infidel Incident, but I do forgive them.

I even forgive them when they must leave me alone. I understand the daily outing to a place called "Work" is required. I've been a latchkey kitty for years, but how I hate the sight of those large rolling cases with zippers.

At first I thought those cases were good fun, jumping right in and taking a nap on the warm fresh clothes, until my parents left for the first time and I was all alone for days, yes days. I still don't understand why I can't be taken along wherever they go. I'm fairly small and I'd fit right in the suitcase.

Unless they're going to The Vet – I don't ever want to go there again. Gosh that's scary. I sure hope they aren't going to The Vet – no, that can't be, nothing about them needs to be fixed.

Of course the house is left well stocked for the times they're away. Dishes are left full and the litter box is clean. When they're gone for more than a couple nights they have a neighbor look in. A neighbor who'll even pet me, but it isn't the same.

They leave me with everything a cat could possibly need, but not what I really want.

In the end, I imagine cats want what everyone really wants – a warm place to sleep where you can feel completely safe, a gentle loving hand to stroke away your sadness, someone to curl up next to when you're lonely, and someone to make you laugh and to laugh with you.

To bask in the warm glow that comes from knowing you're irreplaceable to the ones you love. To know that the ones you love, miss you, as much as you miss them, when they're not with you.

Maybe I did remember the secret of life after all.

Fin & Hart

PARTING WORDS FROM THE "GHOST WRITER"

For the record, I've clearly taken quite a few liberties interpreting what Fin might say if she could. She's a cat after all, and we don't exactly communicate this well. I do think she's pleased with the finished product, as she competed for space with my laptop during the majority of the writing of the book.

I guess I feel qualified to speak on her behalf because I've been a cat interpreter for many years now. I began my long career as cat interpreter when my husband and I met some twenty years ago.

He'd never been around cats, and didn't seem to understand Kirin at all. It was frustrating for both of them. She'd look to me, requesting intervention, and for me to set him straight on the ways of cats. I thought if he could see things from what I imagined was her perspective, they'd learn to live in peace and happiness, and it did help.

When Fin came into our lives, we began speaking to each other on her behalf, and it became a part of our daily conversation. When I'd say "Please fill my dish now Dad!" I meant "Honey, I don't feel like getting up to do it, will you please feed the cat?"

We'd laugh as we'd imagine how the world looked through her eyes. For example, maybe she nibbles me because I taste good, or perhaps because I've broken some unknown cat law and I'm deserving of punishment.

Initially we didn't think she was very bright (she really couldn't figure out how to get the food to come down into the dish). One day, while watching a young starlet claim she was just "playing dumb," it started me down a train of thought.

Perhaps Finny was really brilliant and was just playing dumb to get what she wanted, like so many humans do.

Fin as the semi-intellectual, feline mastermind was born.

The idea for the book began as an assignment in a short story writing class. I wanted something light and humorous to offset the darker side of my writing. I thought a tell-all story, written by a cat about her forbidden love with her toy mouse, would fit the bill. It was the story everyone in class responded to.

The idea then expanded into a book. Maybe being owned by a cat makes you try to put their actions into an understandable human context. I found that speaking as a cat allowed me to poke fun at the foibles of humans while still retaining the heart and humor.

At some point cat ghostwriting became a series of unexpected life lessons.

At first I saw a housecat's world as quite small, when viewed through my eyes. I think anyone who is owned by a housecat has looked at them napping and thought, "I wish I had it so good."

It seems an easy life. On bad days, you could almost resent the life our pets have, when you compare it to your own. Perhaps few lives feel easy to the people who are living them, without the benefit of some perspective.

When I imagined what the world might look like, when viewed through her eyes, I realized it's quite large and filled with the same stresses and joys we all have. The same search to find meaning and purpose, and love and acceptance exists for all of us.

I used to look outside myself to find joy and happiness, acquiring *things* in order to feel satisfaction. I've realized, through Fin's eyes, you don't have to look outside to find joy.

Even a simple life can bring great joy if you appreciate the things you already have within reach.

Fin & Hart

Housecat Confidential

I could hardly let Mom have the last word – It's my book after all. I hope you've enjoyed my tale (or tail).

I offer my deepest thanks to all of you that helped us along the way. You're the best family and friends we could ever hope for.

As for me, I'll be hanging out here with Mousey, keeping things in order and my parents in line, napping and enjoying each day. I hope you find your own patch of sun and someone special to share it with; someone who'll love you no matter what your hair length and always give you a loving scratch under the chin when you need one.

Fin